The Woman On Pier 13

Directed by: Robert Stevenson
Screenplay by: Charles Grayson
and
Robert Hardy Andrews

An Andrew *Velez Book*

FREDERICK UNGAR PUBLISHING CO.
New York

Published by arrangement with RKO General, Inc.

PUBLISHER'S NOTE:

This is the complete final screenplay for the RKO film.
The movie as released may differ from the screenplay
in some respects.

Printed in Great Britain
by Biddles of Guildford

ISBN 0-8044-6880-X

INTRODUCTION

As the decade of the 1950s began, two specters haunted Hollywood. One was the awesome competition from an infant medium: television. The second was Communism. The film industry's response to the threat of losing its heretofore huge and faithful audience was to offer gimmickry in the form of new visual processes. These "wonders" promised to deliver excitement, spectacle, and involvement for the viewer to a degree that could not be matched by the small television screen.

Thus emerged "3-D," "Cinerama," "Vistavision," "Cinemascope," "Superscope," and "Todd-AO." This parade of novel visual forms for the most part soon fell by the wayside cinematically. The end of Hollywood seemed to be at hand, or at least the Hollywood of the all-powerful studio system, which had flourished for over two decades. In its place new sources for films were emerging, including those produced by independent companies and some from abroad – in Europe in particular. All of these efforts were unable to prevent the continuing erosion of audience attendance. People were staying at home en masse to watch "Uncle Miltie" and all the other entertainment they could now have conveniently and free of charge.

In 1950, RKO Radio Pictures for the first time did not have a single picture that earned more than $100,000 in profits. Among the numerous RKO features that ended up "in the red," was *The Woman on Pier 13* or, as it was alternately titled, *I Married a Communist*. After its first disappointing commercial showings, the film was retitled as *The Woman on Pier 13*, in the vain hope that an implication of sex and mystery on the waterfront would stimulate a livelier box-office response than had the terrors of being married to a Communist.

This film was intended to be RKO owner Howard Hughes's personal salvo in the war against the second major horror confronting Hollywood—Communism, specifically Communism in the film industry. This was the year during which Senator Joseph McCarthy of Wisconsin was able to rise from obscurity to a position of awesome national power as the self-proclaimed guardian of America against the "insidious" threat of Communism, in particular in relation to the State Department.

The film industry responded to the investigations by the House Un-American Activities Committee in 1947 by rushing to demonstrate how clean its hands were cinematically. It also established a powerful, if unofficial blacklist, which destroyed many careers and lives. Thus was born a series of artistically shallow and rabidly chauvinistic American pictures such as *The Iron Curtain* (1948), *The Red Danube* and *The Red Menace* (1949) and *I Married a Communist* (1950).

The latter was directed by Robert Stevenson, an RKO "regular," (*Joan of Paris, Walk Softly Stranger*). Set on the San Francisco waterfront, the Marxist heavies in the story are portrayed in much the same style as Depression-era gangsters and wartime-movie Nazis. The hero of the film, portrayed by Robert Ryan, affirms the principle, "better dead than Red," and sacrifices his life to halt the subversive activities of the Party on the waterfront.

During this same year, 1950, Jose Ferrer (*Cyrano de Bergerac*), and Judy Holliday (*Born Yesterday*) became Oscar winners, and a list of films released included *Sunset Boulevard, All About Eve, Father of the Bride, The Men, Samson and Delilah* as well as *Kind Hearts and Coronets* and *Bitter Rice* from abroad. *The Woman on Pier 13* received neither artistic praise nor audience support at the box office. Created out of the trauma of the HUAC's inquisition of Hollywood's writers, (directors and performers) in the late 1940s, it remains today as a museum piece, an odd *noir*-like propaganda document of nearly desperate and simplistic melodrama. From the hindsight of the 1980s, it also offers some unwittingly droll portrayals of relations between the sexes.

The naïve propaganda film continues to surface from time to time. Thus we have John Wayne's *The Green Berets*, supporting without reservation our participation in the Vietnam War, and *Black Like Me*, taking an addlepated sidestep for racial relations. What film gems of a similar nature, one wonders, may emerge from the Reagan 1980s.

Andrew Velez

CAST:

Nan Collins	Laraine Day
Brad Collins	Robert Ryan
Don Lowry	John Agar
Vanning	Thomas Gomez
Christine	Janis Carter
Jim Travis	Richard Rober
Bailey	William Talman
Arnold	Paul E. Burns
Ralston	Paul Guilfoyle
Charles Dover	G. Pat Collins
Grip Wilson	Fred Graham
Mr. Cornwall	Harry Cheshire
Garth	Jack Stoney

CREDITS:

Screenplay	Charles Grayson and
	Robert Hardy Andrews
Story	George W. George and
	George F. Slavin
Executive producer	Sid Rogell
Producer	Jack J. Gross
Director	Robert Stevenson
Director of Photography	Nicholas Musuraca, A.S.C.
Art Directors	Albert S. D'Agostino
	Walter E. Keller
Music	Leigh Harline
Musical Director	C. Bakaleinikoff
Set Decorations	Darrell Silvera
	James Altwies
Film Editor	Roland Gross
Sound	Phil Brigandi
	Clem Portman
Gowns	Michael Woulfe
Hair Styles	Larry Germain

THE WOMAN ON PIER 13
(I MARRIED A COMMUNIST)

FADE IN

EXTERIOR COASTLINE RESORT (STOCK)—DAY
Panning shot establishes ocean, beach, boats offshore, mansions—a luxury hotel.

DISSOLVE THROUGH TO INSERT   HOTEL REGISTER
*A man's hand writes "Bradley Collins and Wife, San Francisco."
A woman's hand takes pen—crosses out "and wife"—puts "Mr. and Mrs." in front of the name.*

INTERIOR HOTEL LOBBY—DAY
A double closeup of Brad and Nan. They're a most attractive couple—with the honeymoon look. Much in love and perfectly attuned, they exchange grins about the business with register.
CLERK'S VOICE: Show Mr. and Mrs. Collins to Suite 17-A.
As they turn

DISSOLVE

INTERIOR HOTEL SUITE—DAY

1

We begin on view through window. Pull back into bedroom—which is done in rococo-moderne. *Suggestion of sitting-room through connecting door—but we don't see into it.*
Through the dissolve, Brad, Nan and a couple of bellboys enter. As dissolve is completed, one bellboy puts luggage on racks, while the other fusses with flowers—then offers key to Brad. He takes key, tips bellboys extravagantly to their visible delight—thumbs them out. When they're alone together, Nan is restive under Brad's frank gaze. She moves to examine flowers.

NAN: Nice.

BRAD: Nothing but the best.

She pretends interest in discovery—indicates vase.

NAN: Ming.

BRAD: Ming who?

NAN: Ming dynasty. Chinese. Of course it's probably not real. *(looks around)* They've really done this very well. Sort of Biedermier mixed with Empire.

BRAD: *(grins)* Honey—don't start educating me again.

Divests her of hat and coat.

BRAD: *(continued)* I told you the first time we fought—you came along 'way too late to change me.

NAN: *(straightforwardly)* I wouldn't want to. But—Brad . . .

BRAD: What?

She hesitates. He draws her down beside him on sofa. His intentions are obvious. She evades.

NAN: Monday—I'm hired to redecorate the offices of the executive vice-president of Cornwall Shipping. Tuesday—I show him my sketches.

BRAD: Chartreuse walls and magenta drapes.

NAN: *(mimicking)* "No woman can do that to me." Big fight.

BRAD: Still fighting Wednesday. Fun, too.

NAN: *(a glance to him)* Thursday, you take me to dinner. Friday you say out of a clear blue sky—"Let's get married."

BRAD: Honey—this is Tuesday . . .

He puts his arm around her.

BRAD: *(continued)* *(grins)* First girl I ever stole from a nice guy. Well—somebody wins—somebody has to lose.

NAN: You're a—very ruthless character.
BRAD: That's the secret of my success.
He starts to kiss her. She buries her head against his shoulder.
BRAD: *(continued)* Hey—honey...!
NAN: *(muffled)* Brad—you—know absolutely nothing about me—really. What I'm really like ...
BRAD: Then it's time I found out.
NAN: I want to be a good wife to you—I—want to be—what you want me to be.
BRAD: *(tips her chin up)* You talk too much.
He kisses her. On their embrace, we

DISSOLVE

INTERIOR COCKTAIL BAR—NIGHT
Full shot. Brad—in white dinner jacket—advances to table in foreground. As he sits, Waiter comes to him.
BRAD: Two champagne cocktails. Use the imported.
CHRISTINE'S VOICE: It used to be "Two Ward 8's"—when we could afford them.
Medium shot of Christine Norman—beautiful, far more "sophisticated" than Nan in dress and manner. Camera pans her to Brad. She's smiling and poised. He's visibly dumbfounded.
CHRISTINE: ... But of course that was when we were very young in dear old Jersey City—before we learned about the finer things in life.
Brad stares grimly during this.
BRAD: *(to Waiter)* Bring the lady a Ward 8.
There's slight emphasis on "lady." Waiter reacts.
BRAD: *(continued)* Three fingers of Bourbon and beer for a chaser.
CHRISTINE: Use the *imported* beer.
Waiter holds chair for her. She sits. Waiter exits.
CHRISTINE: *(continued)* How's the new Mrs. Collins?
BRAD: She's fine. Incidentally—as if you didn't already know—she's joining me any minute.
CHRISTINE: Then I really *ought* to run along.
BRAD: Quit kidding, Christine. Dynamite couldn't blow you out of that chair.

3

CHRISTINE: How right you are. *(pause)* I saw your wedding picture in the papers. She's quite pretty.

BRAD: In her way, you mean.

CHRISTINE: In her way.

BRAD: Which I happen to like.

CHRISTINE: Oh—I'm sure you do. Always knew what you wanted—always got it.

BRAD: Do you know what I'd like to do right now?

CHRISTINE: But the great Bradley Collins can't kick a lady in a public place.

Medium shot delivering Nan just entering. She sees Brad at table with a striking woman—a stranger to her. Camera pans Nan toward them. Seeing her, Brad rises quickly.

BRAD: Nan—this is Christine . . .

CHRISTINE: *(interrupting)* Christine Norman. *(needling Brad)* I'm still single. Odd, isn't it?

NAN: *(as Brad seats her)* The photographer?

CHRISTINE: So nice of you to know. *(to Brad)* You see, I've become famous—too—in my small way. But I imagine you're too busy to read the popular magazines.

During this Waiter enters with the champagne cocktails for Brad and Nan, and Christine's Ward 8—three-ounce whiskey glass, schooner of beer.

Closer shot. This shot is taken with Brad between the two women so we can bounce the scene off his face.

WAITER: *(superciliously)* Your Ward 8, madam.

NAN: What in the world is that?

CHRISTINE: A favorite tipple of the lower classes in Jersey City. Also known as a boilermaker. In the good old days, I used to think your husband invented it.

NAN: Did you, Brad?

BRAD: Don't blame that on *me*.

CHRISTINE: *(lifts both glasses)* Well—here's to three very nice people.

She drinks heartily—without visible effect. Brad and Nan barely sip cocktails.

CHRISTINE: *(continued)* Do you know, Nan—your husband's changed very little—really—after all these years?

NAN: I hope he *never* changes.

CHRISTINE: Charming. A real-life romance. They do happen. *(finishes drink)* Well—I must run along now. I *do* wish I could stay and talk. But we'll meet again—I'm sure. Old friend of family. *(to Brad)* I've just been transferred to San Francisco. The magazine has opened a branch office there.

BRAD: That's great.

CHRISTINE: I knew you'd think so. *(of Nan—to Brad)* She's charming. *(to Nan) So* nice to meet you—Nan. We *must* get together—very soon.

She offers her hand—which Nan perforce accepts. Brad rises perfunctorily.

CHRISTINE: *(continued)* Loved seeing you, Brad.

He doesn't answer.

Closer shot. Brad sits. His eyes follow Christine offstage.

NAN: I'll tell you a secret. I can live the rest of my life without *her.*

BRAD: That makes two of us.

NAN: Mmm. How good *were* the good old days?

BRAD: *No* good, honey. Let's forget.

NAN: I will if you will.

BRAD: *(relaxes; grinning)* Good deal, honey. As far as you and I are concerned—life began last Monday.

NAN: And we go on from there.

Their hands clasp.

FADE OUT

FADE IN

SAN FRANCISCO—DAY—(STOCK)

AN IDENTIFYING SHOT HOLDING THE GOLDEN GATE.

A LARGE APARTMENT HOUSE—(LOCATION)—DAY

INTERIOR CHRISTINE'S LIVING ROOM—DAY
With Christine is a mild-looking man—Arnold—who might be a bank cashier, or accountant, or private investigator. Actually, he owns the J. L. Arnold Storage Warehouse.

ARNOLD: "Born Ann Lowry, Chicago, Illinois. Father—Fred Lowry, architectural draftsman. Mother's maiden name—not known. Both parents deceased . . ."

CHRISTINE: *(interrupts)* When did she come to California?
Arnold scans down the paper, then reads—while Christine is dialing a number on the 'phone.

ARNOLD: ". . . In June, 1945, subject moved to California with her brother. Reason—not known. Worked Masson and Co., decorators. Opened her own establishment January, 1947 . . ."
He breaks off as Christine begins on 'phone.

CHRISTINE: Oh—hello. I have a wedding gift for Mr. and Mrs. Collins. Are they back from their honeymoon yet?

INTERIOR COLLINS' LIVING ROOM—DAY
Don Lowry—Nan's younger brother—husky, good-looking, well-dressed—talks on 'phone. Several beautifully-wrapped wedding gifts are on table near 'phone.
In a section of set, we establish Brad's Union button, cargo-hook he used when he was a stevedore, photos of cargo-crews with Brad as foreman—displayed on wall. Process backing gives effect windows overlook waterfront and bay in distance.

DON: Why—yes—they just got in. *(answering question on 'phone)* Me? Oh—I'm the beautiful bride's brother. Don Lowry.

INTERIOR CHRISTINE'S LIVING ROOM—DAY
She reacts interestedly.

CHRISTINE: Don Lowry?
She gestures impatiently to Arnold—who hands her one of the other papers he holds.

INSERT PAPER.
It is divided into headings:
Occupation

6

Religious Affiliations
Education, etc.
We hold only to read the name Don Lowry *at the top and get*
general impression of the document.
CHRISTINE'S VOICE: Oh—*my* name wouldn't mean a thing to you.
We've never met.

INTERIOR COLLINS' LIVING ROOM—DAY
Close on Don—likeably intrigued.
DON: We *should.* That voice *has* to have a beautiful face. *(listens
again)* You sound like a blonde. But I'll settle for a brunette.

INTERIOR CHRISTINE'S LIVING ROOM—DAY
Close on Christine.
CHRISTINE: But you'd rather have a blonde.
As she speaks, she looks down at the paper.

INSERT PAPER
One paragraph about Don is headed:
"Character"
The entry includes the word:
"Impressionable"
Christine's pencil underlines this word.
CHRISTINE'S VOICE: What do *you* do, Mr. Lowry? Besides talk on
telephones? *(pause)* Oh, I see. That sounds very interesting.

INTERIOR COLLINS' LIVING ROOM—DAY
Don at 'phone.
DON: *I'm* interested in *you.* "Guess who's" a fine game—but let's
not overdo it.

INTERIOR CHRISTINE'S LIVING ROOM—DAY
CHRISTINE: *(she's been through this before)* No—I think I'll keep us
both in suspense for a while. *(against protest) Loved* talking to you—
Mr. Lowry.
She checks document Arnold gave her.
CHRISTINE: *(continued)* I thought this was supposed to be complete.

On Arnold's reaction.

CHRISTINE: *(continued)* He says he's been working as a stevedore the last two weeks. Mr. Collins got him the job. *(crisply)* Did the file on Collins come in?

Arnold hands her a roll of microfilm.

ARNOLD: I wonder sometimes why everything has to be on microfilm.

As he speaks, Christine walks toward door of her kitchenette—which has been converted into darkroom.

CHRISTINE: *(as she goes)* When I have time—I'll explain it to you.

Arnold—definitely put in his place—follows her.

INTERIOR COLLINS' LIVING ROOM—DAY

Don is unwrapping a wedding gift. Nan appears on balcony—comes down the stairs.

NAN: Did the 'phone ring a few minutes ago?

DON: Somebody else about some more loot for the bride.

NAN: Who?

DON: That I would like to know.

As he speaks, he takes from box a striking Chinese vase.

NAN: *(calls delightedly)* Brad!

Brad appears from bedroom above—has changed, and ties neck-tie, buttons coat, as he comes down stairs and to Nan.

NAN: *(continued)* Brad! Ming! Real—this time!

BRAD: Now—we're not going to go through all that again.

She sets vase on mantelpiece near Brad's cargo-hook.

DON: *(reads card that came with gift)* From—no less than Mr. and Mrs. J. Francis Cornwall.

Obviously, Cornwall is important to Brad.

BRAD: *(grins)* If the boss likes it—*I* like it. So we'll keep it.

He takes vase from mantelpiece—hands it to her firmly.

BRAD: *(continued)* In the closet out of my sight. To be brought out only when the Cornwalls come to call.

Sound of distant tug-whistles come offstage. At once, Brad looks from window. We do not see what he sees.

BRAD: *(continued)* The *Nellie J.'s* in from Shanghai. Rush cargo—three days overdue.

DON: *(a side-look at Nan)* Now—how can you tell what ship it is from here?

BRAD: How can you use a cargo-hook on her from here?

DON: *(grins; unabashed)* I can't. Which makes me very happy. *(at Brad's half-grim look)* Look—boss—I'm taking a day off. Special event—you and Nan ...

BRAD: *(fake-tough) Get over there!*

He grins but means what he says. Don takes it grinningly.

DON: *(turning to go)* Okay, boss—okay. I'm on my way!

He shows palms of hands to Nan.

DON: *(continued)* Look—already—blisters on top of blisters.

BRAD: After a while it'll be callouses on top of callouses!

DON: *(has reached door)* "And you'll be a man, my son!"

He exits grinningly. Door bangs.

Close on Nan and Brad.

NAN: And the funny thing is—he's right. You've done more to make a man of Don in a few weeks than I was able to do in twenty-four years.

Suddenly, she puts her arms around Brad.

NAN: *(continued)* You're quite a man yourself—Mr. Collins.

BRAD: Keep right on believing that—honey.

On their kiss, we

DISSOLVE THROUGH TO INTERIOR CHRISTINE'S APARTMENT—DARKROOM—DAY

INSERT

Darkroom tray. Christine's hands slosh photo print in tray. We reveal enlarged photo of Brad and Christine when they were younger. They're in swimming suits—photographed on the beach. Brad's arm is around her waist. They're laughing—very obviously, are sweethearts.

Close on Christine with Arnold at her elbow. She stares at photograph. For first time since we've known her, sincere emotion shows on her face. She's bitter—resentful—unhappy.

ARNOLD: You made a handsome couple.

9

Christine doesn't even hear him. She starts drying print with roller. During this, we go to
Big head of Christine. Her face is eloquent with memories. We should almost pity her.

FADE OUT

FADE IN

EXTERIOR OF A SHIPPING OFFICE ON THE EMBAR-
CADERO AT SAN FRANCISCO—DAY—(STOCK)
We matte in the name "Cornwall Shipping Company." This should be a shot with plenty of activity, and preferably a ship being loaded in the background.

DISSOLVE

A DOOR—MARKED:
BRADLEY COLLINS
EXECUTIVE VICE-PRESIDENT

DISSOLVE

INTERIOR BRAD'S OFFICE—DAY
Close on Brad—who is half-turned from camera, looking out and down through window. By suggestion, he surveys the waterfront activity in which he's a highly important cog.
JIM TRAVIS'S VOICE: . . . So that's why we came to you, Brad. When we start negotiating the new contract, we don't want the usual schlemozzle—because that might end up in a waterfront tieup—and the union doesn't want that any more than you owners want it. So this time we'd like to find out what happens if both sides work together right from the start.
During this, camera pulls back—revealing three labor leaders who've come for private conference with Brad. Jim Travis—the spokesman—is as big as Brad, tough, smart and honest. Charlie

10

NAMELESS, SHAMELESS WOMAN!
Trained in an art
as old as time—
I MARRIED a Communist

RKO
RADIO
PICTURES

PANTAGES
HOLLYWOOD
★
RKO
HILLSTREET

STARTS
SATURDAY
OCT. 8

NAMELESS, SHAMELESS WOMAN!
Trained in an art as old as time!

RKO
presents

I MARRIED a
Communist

LARAINE DAY • ROBERT RYAN
JOHN AGAR
with THOMAS GOMEZ • JANIS CARTER

SID ROGELL • JACK J. GROSS • ROBERT STEVENSON

Dover is equally straightforward on the surface. The third labor leader is Ed Hagen.

JIM: Our suggestion is a small committee—labor men who know the score—management men who'll kick the ball back and forth with us 'til we get a contract worked out that's fair all around.

BRAD: You know I can't speak for the owners, Jim.

JIM: You can speak *to* 'em. And they'll listen to you. How about it, Brad?

BRAD: *(moves in; crisply)* It makes a lot of sense. I'll put it up to the right people—recommend it—try to get an okay. Okay with you?

JIM: *(grins)* Gotta be. Since we brought it up. *(to others)* Anything you want to add?

Charlie Dover and Hagen shake their heads—prepare to go.

HAGEN: Good seein' you, Brad.

BRAD: Same to you, Ed. How's the new *bambino?*

HAGEN: Best-lookin' kid you ever saw.

BRAD: Must take after its mother.

Hagen grins—fakes punch at Brad's ribs—exits.

CHARLIE DOVER: *(to Jim)* You comin' or staying?

JIM: I'll be along in a minute, Charlie.

DOVER: Okay. So long, Brad.

BRAD: See you, Charlie.

Charlie Dover exits.

Close on Brad and Jim near mantelpiece on which there's a model of one of the Cornwall cargo-ships. Also in shot is a framed photograph of Nan. The men stand so that while neither looks at the picture, Nan is nevertheless present during their talk.

BRAD: I'm—glad you came in with this proposition, Jim.

JIM: Well—we came to the right man with it.

BRAD: We'll have no trouble.

JIM: No reason why we should have.

There's possible double meaning in this. Brad pursues.

BRAD: That's business. Now about us.

JIM: I knew Nan three years. You knew her a week. She married you—not me. That's it. Just don't let her regret anything.

BRAD: I won't. *(pause)* She'd feel fine if you'd drop in and see us.

JIM: I'll do that. Soon as we get this contract squared away.

11

They exchange look of understanding—two pretty good men who've settled a difficult personal matter in a sensible and friendly way—and start out together.

INTERIOR BRAD'S OUTER OFFICE—DAY
This shot is taken over shoulder of a man—Nixon—in foreground with back to camera. Brad and Jim emerge together from inner office. Brad's Secretary is at her desk off at side.
BRAD: Be seeing you soon, then, Jim.
JIM: *(exiting)* Sure. My best to Nan.
Brad turns to go back into inner office.
NIXON: *(starts forward)* Oh—Mr. Collins . . .
Brad stops. Nixon moves to him.
NIXON: *(continued) (pleasantly apologetic)* I'd be very grateful for a few moments of your time, Mr. Collins. It's about an article I'm writing.
Close on Brad and Nixon—who wears horn-rimmed spectacles, is neatly but not obtrusively well-dressed, and carries briefcase. His manner and speech are those of an educated, rather modest man.
BRAD: I'm pretty busy right now.
NIXON: I know. But—as a matter of fact, Mr. Collins—the article is principally about *you.*
Brad has a streak of healthy vanity—responds to this.
BRAD: Come on in.
Nixon enters inner office ahead of Brad.

INTERIOR BRAD'S OFFICE—DAY
Nixon surveys surroundings admiringly while he speaks.
NIXON: My name is Nixon. My specialty is the American success story. *(smiles—crossing office)* This office certainly spells success, Mr. Collins. *(continuing toward window)* . . . And the man who wields such power—was once only a simple stevedore . . . *(he reaches window; indicates from it)* . . . Like all those men working down there. What a wonderful advertisement for the American system of free enterprise!

12

He has put down his briefcase near Brad's desk. Now he produces leather cigarette-case—offers cigarette to Brad, who declines silently but snaps gold lighter to give Nixon a light.

NIXON: *(continued)* Thank you, Mr. Collins. *(of lighter)* Gold. Beautiful. A symbol—no doubt.

BRAD: A present from my wife. *(briskly)* Now—what do you want to know?

Nixon sits—opens briefcase—rummages through folders.

NIXON: *(during this action)* I'm a student of contrasts. They're what makes this country of ours so fabulous to the rest of the world. *(finds what he seeks)* On one hand, we have Mr. Bradley Collins—the great success story. On the other—here I have the record of a very unsuccessful young man named Frank Johnson.

Brad shows no visible reaction—asks:

BRAD: Who's he?

NIXON: He was typical of the lost generation—produced by the depression in the '30's. He left school—ambitious, strong, intelligent—hunting a job, to make his start up the ladder. Unfortunately—there *were* no jobs.

BRAD: *(calmly)* Why tell *me* about him?

NIXON: I'm coming to that—Mr. Collins. *(consults documents)* Embittered—and violent by nature—Frank Johnson joined the Young Communists' League—then became a full-fledged member of the Party ... *(seems to skip through document—hitting only the salient details)* ... Party card listed *Frank J.* ... Agit-prop activities, strikes in New Jersey ... Very prominent in strong-arm work ... Then suddenly—broke all connections with the Party and disappeared ... Reason unknown ...

He stops—puts folder down—removes spectacles in a gesture we'll learn is characteristic. With spectacles off, Nixon is a changed man: cold, hard, the complete "intellectual."

NIXON: *(continued)* ... Or it *was* unknown until now. But now it's obvious—isn't it, Johnson?

No reaction from Brad.

NIXON: *(continued)* You decided you might do better for yourself. Having used the Party for all you could get out of it, you betrayed

13

your Party oath—disappeared . . . came to the West Coast . . . and as Bradley Collins you *have* done better—for *yourself.*

During this, Brad tightens but betrays nothing.

BRAD: Don't you know it's dangerous to call anybody a Communist—unless you can prove it?

NIXON: Christine Norman can prove it.

Brad takes this like a body blow.

NIXON: *(continued)* Please, Johnson—let's not have any loud denials or threats that will waste your time and mine. Christine Norman has a remarkable memory for faces. Also—she kept photographs—as women in love do.

BRAD: All right. How much do you want?

NIXON: This isn't blackmail, Johnson.

BRAD: *(grimly)* Then you're out of luck. I might do business with a blackmailer. Not with a Party agent. Not now or any other time.

Nixon studies him—visibly unaffected by Brad's defiance.

BRAD: *(continued)* Now get out—and stay out.

NIXON: Very well—Johnson.

Unhurriedly, he dons spectacles—closes a briefcase. As if in casual afterthought, he drops a card on desk.

NIXON: *(continued)* By the way—this has been brought up to date for you.

Again in the pose of mild-mannered journalist, he crosses and opens door. Brad stands staring after him. Door closes.

Close on Brad. Slowly, he picks up the card Nixon left. He stares at it bitterly.

INSERT CARD
An authentic Party card dated 1949—*filled out to* Frank J. *Brad's fist closes, crumpling card.*

DISSOLVE THROUGH TO INTERIOR CHRISTINE'S LIVING ROOM—DAY
Christine—in striking negligee—comes from bedroom to ringing 'phone. She cuts ring—answering.

CHRISTINE: Yes? *(reacts oddly)* Who? Oh. *(pause; deciding)* All right. Let him come up.

14

INTERIOR LOBBY OF CHRISTINE'S APARTMENT—
DAY
Brad—wearing hat but no coat—enters elevator.

INTERIOR CHRISTINE'S LIVING ROOM—DAY
Christine smiles oddly—not mirthfully—as she moves to side-board, gets bottles and glasses.

INTERIOR CORRIDOR—DAY
Brad comes from elevator—sets himself before ringing Christine's bell.

INTERIOR CHRISTINE'S LIVING ROOM—DAY
Christine is just ending the pouring of two Ward 8's—as doorbell buzzes. Significantly, she places drinks on coffee-table before crossing to open the door. She faces Brad.
CHRISTINE: *(with surface lightness)* Welcome—stranger. Come in—come in.
She takes his hat—tosses it on chair near door. Whatever's in Brad's mind—and we're not sure yet what he's driving at—he moves with her to coffee-table and sofa.
CHRISTINE: *(continued) (indicates drinks)* You see—I'm still the sentimental type—deep down underneath.
BRAD: That's what I was wondering about.
He lifts his drinks. She does the same.
CHRISTINE: Salute to yesterday.
Brad drinks with her. She disposes herself on sofa. He appraises her. After pause, he takes crumpled Party card from pocket—tosses it on coffee-table toward her.
BRAD: A friend of yours brought that to me. I thought I'd drop over and ask you—why? What for?
She shrugs noncommittally—awaits his next move.
BRAD: *(continued)* Just to sink the knife in me—after so long? Kind of silly for a smart girl like you. *(half-grins)* So I walked out on you. So I figured you got as much as you gave, while it lasted.
CHRISTINE: Did I?
BRAD: Sure. We started even and quit the same way.

15

He sets drinks down—studies her—still grins.

BRAD: *(continued)* Baby—you didn't sic your friend on me just to pay off for the past. Uh-uh.

Christine makes us feel she's not too sure, herself.

CHRISTINE: *(slowly; eyes on him)* There's an old saying. We live today. Can't change yesterday. Can't do *much* about today. Tomorrow—who knows?

BRAD: I gotta remember that.

Deliberately—proceeding with a plan—he sits beside her.

BRAD: *(continued) (from this vantage)* You know—put us side by side—we still look pretty good.

CHRISTINE: *(beginning to go for it)* I—used to like Frank Johnson.

BRAD: So you used to tell me. *(arm along sofa-back)* What've you got against Bradley Collins? Same man. Few years older. But not *too* old.

CHRISTINE: *(half-laughs—but with a catch in her voice)* Still the—hairy-chested physical type.

BRAD: Is that bad?

CHRISTINE: There was a time when it was fine.

BRAD: Not so long ago.

CHRISTINE: Not—so long ago—at that.

She sways to him—hands on his shoulders. He doesn't meet her halfway. His motionless reaction is like a slap in her face.

BRAD: *(grins contemptuously)* I wondered if it was Party or personal. Well—now I know.

She freezes as he speaks—staring at him. He stands.

BRAD: *(continued) (quiet but searing)* You had an idea you could yank me back in the Party—and if you could do that you *might* be able to yank me back to you. Part-time, anyhow. No dice—baby. I can't use you.

She comes up raging.

BRAD: *(continued)* I graduated from you—a long time back. *(picks up Party card)* Same time I graduated from this. *(flips it to fall at her feet)* Paste it in your scrapbook, baby—among your many souvenirs.

He turns from her, gets hat, starts to exit.

Shot over Christine. Trembling with insulted fury, she bends suddenly—throws the Ward 8 glasses at Brad just as he opens door. As if he anticipated this move—knowing her of old—he

16

moves door just enough so glasses shatter against it, missing him.
He grins back at her insultingly as he exits. Door closes.
Close on Christine. If she could kill Brad, she would.

DISSOLVE

INTERIOR COLLINS' LIVING ROOM—NIGHT
Closeup of the Ming vase—held in the frail, aristocratic hands of
Cornwall, Brad's boss and friend.
CORNWALL'S VOICE: ... This is very interesting to me, Brad—and I
hope to you. Very beautiful—rather rare—quite useless ... The
ultimate achievement of a feudal system at its peak ...
During this, camera pulls back—revealing Brad and Cornwall
seated in foreground. Cornwall is white-haired, dignified—admi-
rable. Both men wear dinner-jackets.
In background is a group of which Nan is the center: solid-looking
folk—San Francisco shipping men and their wives, all in evening
clothes. Dinner is over. Four people play bridge. The others talk.
Here's wealth at its best.
CORNWALL: ... And—I suppose—I'm the product of an outmoded
feudal system, too. *(sets vase down)* While you're the product of a new
system, a new world ...
'Phone rings at Brad's elbow.
BRAD: Excuse me, Mr. Cornwall. *(answers on 'phone)* Yes?

INTERIOR 'PHONE BOOTH—NIGHT
Effect is that this is in first-floor lobby of apartment building in
which Brad and Nan live. Bailey—a flashy, conceited piecework
killer—speaks on 'phone. Grip Wilson—Bailey's towering fol-
lower—is close by. Flight of stairs rises in background.
BAILEY: *(on 'phone)* This Frank Johnson? *(sardonic)* Okay—so it's
Mr. Collins! Nixon wants you. We got a car down here waiting.

INTERIOR COLLINS' LIVING ROOM—NIGHT
For good reasons, Brad keeps his face away from Cornwall while
he speaks on 'phone.
BRAD: Look—I've got guests. I can't possibly leave now. No.

17

During this, Nan approaches from background. As Brad hangs up, she speaks to Cornwall:

NAN: Could I get you a liqueur, Mr. Cornwall?

He rises courteously as she speaks. Brad follows suit.

CORNWALL: Something mild. Doctor's orders. Also Mrs. Cornwall's.

She smiles—leaves them.

CORNWALL: *(continued)* Fine. Fine. She's what you needed, Brad. From now on—you're all set.

BRAD: *(oddly)* I've been lucky so far.

CORNWALL: Not a question of luck. Man decides what he wants in his life—goes after it—gets it—you can't call that 'luck'—

He sits down again—grins at Brad's reaction.

CORNWALL: *(continued)* Which leads right into what I wanted to talk to you about. The owners have talked over your recommendations about the new contract. We've decided to dump the whole thing right into your lap.

BRAD: *(honestly taken aback)* Now—wait a minute, Mr. Cornwall . . .

CORNWALL: Oh—you'll have a committee. But you're the chairman.

Under other circumstances, this would mean much to Brad. As it is, he feels he must temporize.

CORNWALL: *(continued)* The Union leaders talk your language— and you talk theirs. Because you came up the hard way—they respect you. So do the owners.

BRAD: Well—when you put it that way . . .

CORNWALL: You accept the nomination! *(smiles)* So it's your baby. Just don't forget we have to pay dividends. Widows and orphans, you know.

BRAD: *(grins)* Jim Travis will leave us a couple of bucks for them.

CORNWALL: I hope so. I'm one of the orphans.

Nan has entered during this. She brings tray with two balloon glasses. Cornwall takes his smilingly. Brad is about to follow suit when door-buzzer sounds.

BRAD: *(reacts with reason; quickly to Nan)* Excuse me.

NAN: I'll get it, Brad.

BRAD: *(moving away)* Let *me* do a little work for a change.
He continues to the door.

INTERIOR LOBBY OF COLLINS' HOME—NIGHT
Brad opens door—reacts when he faces Bailey and sees Grip glowering in background.
BAILEY: Mr. Collins?
BRAD: Yes.
BAILEY: I guess you don't hear so good on the 'phone. I'll say it real slow and plain. Nixon wants you. So come on.
BRAD: Now—look . . .
BAILEY: You wouldn't want us to cause a commotion in front of your guests.
Brad controls his anger. Bailey smirks.
BAILEY: *(continued)* I like a guy that listens to reason. *(indicates)* Better get a shawl. That monkey-suit's kind of fancy for where we're goin'.
BRAD: All right. With you in a minute.
BAILEY: *(as Brad closes door)* Make it a *short* minute.
Brad is opening closet to get his hat and coat when Nan enters from living room.
NAN: What is it?
BRAD: *(improvising quickly)* Oh—a foul-up down at the docks—one of our ships.
NAN: That sounds serious.
BRAD: I'll know when I get there. *(indicating offstage)* I—don't want to break up the party. I'll just duck out and get back quick as I can. *(on the move)* Have to hurry, honey.
Suddenly he stops—kisses her hard. Releasing her, he gives her a strange look that puzzles her. He exits quickly. Door closes. Nan doesn't see Bailey and Grip.
Close on Nan. She's obscurely disturbed. But she shakes it off—turns to rejoin the guests as we

DISSOLVE

EXTERIOR COLLINS' APARTMENT BUILDING—NIGHT

In long shot we see Bailey and Grip lead Brad to waiting black sedan. They get in, and the car drives off.

DISSOLVE

EXTERIOR WATERFRONT (BETHLEHEM STEEL)—NIGHT
We begin on ripples of light in the water as it laps against the piles of a wooden jetty, then, as light increases, pan up to show the black sedan approaching along a bleak and deserted section of the waterfront.
Through a maze of cranes, the sedan swings around and comes to rest in front of a metal roller door.

DOORKEEPER'S BOX (BETHLEHEM STEEL)—NIGHT
A lookout—Burke—peers through window—flashes a light— then moves over to open the roller door.

INTERIOR WAREHOUSE (BETHLEHEM STEEL)—NIGHT
Bailey and Grip lead Brad in from the sedan. Grip closes the heavy door. Elevator begins to rise.

INTERIOR WELL OF WAREHOUSE (BETHLEHEM STEEL)—NIGHT
Paralleling the motion of the elevator, the camera tilts up in a striking shot over the maze of girders and floors.

INTERIOR FOURTH FLOOR OF WAREHOUSE (BETHLEHEM STEEL)—NIGHT
Elevator arrives. Bailey and Grip lead Brad across corridor. Bales and boxes are in shadowed background. A couple of cargo-hooks are spiked in bales. We make no point of these at this time.
Bailey knocks on door. A typical bodyguard—Garth—opens door.
BAILEY: *(to Garth)* Collins.
Garth indicates for Brad to enter—enters behind him, closing door on Bailey and Grip.

20

INTERIOR PARTY ROOM (STUDIO)—NIGHT

Nixon is seated at table. His spectacles are off. Facing him is a meager, frightened man—Ralston. Arnold takes notes. Room is bare—just table and a few chairs.
No evident attention is paid to Brad. Garth leans against wall in background.
Ralston—frightened, desperate—defends with mounting hysteria against passionless interrogation.

RALSTON: I don't care what you were told—Mr. Nixon, It's not true. Someone has made a terrible mistake . . .

NIXON: *(interrupts)* The mistake was yours—to be seen coming out of the F.B.I. office.

RALSTON: No—no! I don't even know where their office is! I—I may have just *passed* it without knowing . . .

NIXON: *(interrupts again)* Then how do you account for Drobny being picked up the next day? You were his only contact.

RALSTON: Maybe they trailed him from Los Angeles—maybe he got drunk and talked too much—*I* don't know. . . ! But *I* never . . .

NIXON: *(again interrupts)* Strange—isn't it?—how a man will try to turn against his friends, and believe he can get away with it?

Ralston cringes; Nixon speaks curtly to Garth:

NIXON: *(continued)* Take him out.

Garth moves with robot-like efficiency—gripping Ralston—forcing him out. Door opened for moment shows us Bailey and Grip in background outside. Door closes.

NIXON: *(exactly as before)* All right, Johnson.

Brad advances to him grimly.

BRAD: I came down here to get something settled . . .

NIXON: *(interrupts—just as he interrupted Ralston)* I *sent* for you—Johnson—because I wanted to refresh your memory about what can happen to Party members who betray their Party oath. In *your* case, you're going to be given the opportunity to redeem yourself . . .

BRAD: Look—I'm *out* of the Party. I've been out for years. You've got nothing *I* want . . . What do you want from *me*?

As he speaks, Nixon dons spectacles—writes on slip of paper. Brad's half-plea, half-challenge means nothing.

21

NIXON: *(interrupting again)* Beginning immediately, two-fifths of your salary will be deposited in this bank, to the account of this organization. *(hands slip across table)* The organization is listed as a charity. Therefore, your contributions are tax-deductible. That's very important to some of our higher-bracket members. Incidentally—Johnson—we know the exact amount of your income from all sources.

BRAD: I *bet* you do! Just like the good old days.

NIXON: Not quite. Frank Johnson could make speeches at meetings—pass out handbills—brawl in the streets. Mr. Bradley Collins can't. Your present position qualifies you for much more important service to the Party.

BRAD: Now—look ...

NIXON: *(interrupts; exactly as to Ralston)* You'll be notified when I have orders for you. That's all.

He turns away to some papers on table.

BRAD: Now let me tell *you* something! I quit taking orders a long time back. And if you crowd me too hard—I'll kick the whole thing over. And if I have to start punching—I'll start at the top. Is that clear?

NIXON: Quite clear. You can go back to your dinner-guests now, Johnson.

Brad hesitates—wants to throw punches. Slowly—burning up inside—he turns and exits.

INTERIOR FOURTH FLOOR WAREHOUSE (BETHLEHEM STEEL)—NIGHT

Brad comes from Party Room—crosses to elevator and enters it. Before he can close the heavy door, Arnold hurries from the Party Room—speaks as he enters elevator:

ARNOLD: I'm to show you the way out.

Brad gives him a look. Door closes. Elevator starts down.

WIPE

EXTERIOR WHARF (BETHLEHEM STEEL)—NIGHT

22

Brad and Arnold come out of shadows and approach a huge traveling crane. Arnold produces cigarette—stops in foreground.

ARNOLD: Have you a match?

Grimly, Brad produces his gold lighter—snaps it. Arnold puffs—blows out the flame. Brad snaps lighter again. Arnold inhales and puffs—causing flame to flare high. Actually, he uses this to provide a signal.

Suddenly—out of darkness—Bailey and Grip appear herding a prisoner we recognize as Ralston. Agony and terror show on his face.

The camera pans with them but remains on Brad and Arnold when it reaches them.

EXTERIOR PIER (BETHLEHEM STEEL)—NIGHT

Bailey and Grip hustle Ralston along the pier until they disappear into the darkness.

A moment later there's the sound of a heavy blow—then the sound of a body falling from pier into the water.

Almost at once, Bailey and Grip emerge from darkness alone. Close shot of Arnold and Brad. Arnold watches for Brad's reaction to murder staged for his benefit.

BRAD: *(curtly)* All right. Tell Nixon I saw what he wanted me to see—*and I think it stinks. Now I'll find my own way out.*

His fury startles Arnold. Brad exits—leaving Arnold staring.

DISSOLVE

EXTERIOR WHARF (STUDIO)—NIGHT

The set is dark, desolate, evil. A figure appears from shadows—moves quickly to telephone box set between two buildings.

Close shot at telephone box—revealing that the figure is Brad. Booth has no door. Brad dials a number quickly. Before he gets an answer:

NIXON'S VOICE: Johnson.

Brad half-turns into camera.

23

Nixon's Voice: *(continued)* Before you talk to the Police, Johnson—there are several details you ought to know about. That's why I followed you.

Voice over 'Phone: Police Department. Hello. Police Department.

Slowly, Brad hangs up—cutting voice. As he steps from booth, camera pulls back—for first time revealing Nixon.

Nixon: You're much too impetuous for a supposedly intelligent man.

Brad is taut—anything but a beaten victim at this point.

Nixon: *(continued)* The Police might try to protect you—in return for information. But in that case—naturally—we'd have to deliver your Party record to your employers.

Surprisingly to us—and to Nixon—Brad grins grimly.

Brad: I got news for you. I'm going to tell 'em myself. I won't be the first sucker who got into the Party—and got smart—and got out. And probably I won't be the last.

Big closeup of Nixon. He listens studiously—unaffected.

Brad's voice: But I know my people better than you do. If I'm on the level with *them* there's a fifty-fifty chance they'll give me a break.

Close on Brad—over Nixon.

Brad: That's fifty percent better odds than I'd get from the dear old Party. So if you're so anxious for a showdown—come on. We'll walk over to the nearest Police station together. And I'll take it from there and you do the same.

Nixon: No, Johnson. You *might* be as brave as you sound—brave enough to risk losing everything you've achieved. But I doubt if you're brave enough to send yourself to the electric chair—for murder.

Brad takes this like a blow to the body.

Nixon: *(continued)* You remember very well. That shop-steward who was killed in a street fight in New Jersey. The case was never cleared up.

As he speaks, he takes photostat print from his pocket. He offers this toward Brad. During ensuing, Brad takes it.

Nixon: *(continued)* This is the photostat of a Party report—in your handwriting—giving complete details of the killing. The original is on file at New York headquarters—and will be mailed to the Police here if necessary.

Closeup of Brad. Now for the first time he's whipped.

NIXON'S VOICE: I hope it won't be necessary. However—that's for you to decide.

Shot over Brad—whose face is out of camera.

NIXON: *(turning to go)* Good night, Johnson.

We hold as Nixon walks away along dark passage, and slowly

DISSOLVE THROUGH TO INTERIOR COLLINS' LIVING ROOM—NIGHT

Starting in closeup of the photostat print being consumed by flames in fireplace.

Camera pans up—angle widens—revealing Brad's tortured, oddly-lighted face as he stares down at the fire. No other light in shot. Significantly, Brad's cargo-hook and other trophies of success are on wall near him.

Brad strikes balled fist in palm. Slowly, he exits and starts up the stairs.

INTERIOR COLLINS' BEDROOM—NIGHT

Nan's in bed and asleep. She has been reading—dozed off with bedside lamp lighted. Brad—entering—reacts to this picture. He moves to her quietly—stands looking down at her. Most of all, he dreads losing Nan. Slowly, we

FADE OUT

FADE IN

INTERIOR CHRISTINE'S LIVING ROOM—NIGHT

We start in closeup of photo layout in a magazine—somewhat in Life *or* Look *format, but not too similar—headed something like* "They Move Mountains of Cargo with Their Bare Hands: A Photo-Story by Christine Norman."

The photos are stills of stevedores at work, using cargo-hooks.
Featured is Don—stripped to the waist, muscular and smilingly
attractive.

CHRISTINE'S VOICE: *(lightly; she speaks on phone)* Oh—hello, Don.
Eight? You'd better make it nine. I'm a working woman—and it
takes time to get out of my overalls and into something fresh and
feminine . . .

During this, camera pulls back over Nixon's shoulder—revealing
that he studies picture in magazine while Christine talks on
'phone. Again, she's in a smart negligee.

CHRISTINE: *(laughing at something Don says on 'phone)* Oh—you
would, would you? We'll discuss that later. *(briskly)* Nine—and in the
lobby. 'Bye now, darling.

She hangs up. Nixon tosses magazine aside

NIXON: *(echoes)* "Darling."

CHRISTINE: *(challenging)* Do you mind?

NIXON: *(ignores this)* How did you meet him?

CHRISTINE: Oh—talked to him on the 'phone by accident. He liked
my voice. So I talked to him again . . .

NIXON: *Not* by accident . . .

CHRISTINE: . . . And I told him I liked *his* voice.

NIXON: Why? Now you've got him running after you.

CHRISTINE: Oh—call it a whim.

NIXON: We'll call it what it is. You're trying to annoy Johnson—just
for the emotional satisfaction it gives you.

CHRISTINE: *(pointedly)* And emotion is something you're not built to
understand, approve of—or appreciate. *(challenging)* And just for
the record—I don't have to work for the Party twenty-four hours a
day.

NIXON: I will decide what you have to do. *(pause)* You've been given
important responsibilities in the Party apparatus. They must not be
prejudiced by personal entanglements.

Christine gives an irritated laugh.

CHRISTINE: The bureau contact in Detroit had different ideas.
(smiles pointedly) I might say he had *very* different ideas.

NIXON: Perhaps that's why he was replaced.

Christine starts to speak—but catches herself. She exits suddenly to bedroom—slamming door.
Closeup of Nixon—coldly thoughtful about her conduct.

DISSOLVE
Close shot—a little cake.
Waiter places cake with one small candle on table.
WAITER'S VOICE: May I offer my congratulations on the first year . . . ?
MAN'S VOICE: The first *month*.

INTERIOR NIGHTCLUB—NIGHT
An intimate spot—tastefully done. Smartly-dressed people are at other tables, or dancing to music of small orchestra. Brad and Nan are at table in foreground.
BRAD: And we accept the congratulations.
At Brad's look, Waiter exits understandingly.
NAN: *(bends toward candle; singsong style)* I wish—I wish—I wish!
She blows out the candle.
BRAD: What?
NAN: Woman stuff. You wouldn't understand.
BRAD: Want to bet?
She shakes her head smilingly—then sobers, studying him.
NAN: Brad—are you really as happy as I am?
BRAD: Any reason why I shouldn't be?
NAN: I—don't know. You've seemed—well, worried lately.
Brad's face clouds. He tries to cover.
BRAD: Just things going wrong at the office. Man stuff, honey.
To change subject, he looks at wristwatch, and asks:
BRAD: *(continued)* Wonder what's keeping Don?
NAN: Oh—new girl. Probably briefing her before she meets the old folks.
BRAD: Who is she?
NAN: He didn't say. She must be somebody very special, though. He got a haircut two days early—just for her benefit.
During this, she hasn't abandoned the original topic of her real interest. Now she returns to it.

27

NAN: *(continued)* Brad—I wish you'd tell me what's bothering you so much. Maybe I couldn't help—but I'd try.

Brad's reaction startles her. He speaks almost harshly:

BRAD: Look—we came out to try and have a good time. Shall we let it go at that?

Nan's eyes widen. Brad looks from her—offstage. There's a moment of silence between them. Then Brad is visibly startled by what he sees:

Shot of Don approaching—with Christine.

NAN: *(as surprised as Brad)* Oh—no—not *her!*

Camera pans Don and Christine to table. Brad rises grimly.

DON: Hi, Nan—Brad. Christine Norman—my sister—my brother-in-law . . .

BRAD: *(tight-lipped)* We've met.

DON: I know, but I like to introduce people. Swell start for the conversation.

He's unaware of anything wrong—places chair for Christine. She sits. He moves in close beside her.

CHRISTINE: So *nice,* seeing you both again.

BRAD: *(almost as she speaks)* Waiter! *(to Don)* What'll you have?

DON: Two Ward 8's.

Brad and Nan react to this.

BRAD: I thought you were on the wagon.

DON: I—fell off.

CHRISTINE: He didn't fall. He was pushed.

Waiter enters during this.

BRAD: *(to Waiter)* Two Ward 8's. Three fingers of bourbon—beer on the side.

Waiter takes this—exits as Christine affects to notice the small cake for first time, and picks it up.

CHRISTINE: How charming! The first anniversary. A whole month! *(smiling to Nan)* He *is* the steadfast type—after all. Do you know, Nan—I *like* the men in your life?

NAN: *(pretty well fed up)* Do you know—so do I.

She rises.

NAN: *(continued)* Come on, Don—dance with me.

Don reacts—rises.

28

DON: *(to Christine)* Excuse—please.
He exits with Nan.
Close on Brad and Christine. He's burning. She won't look at him—smiles triumphantly while her eyes follow Don offstage. Moving shot of Nan and Don dancing.
DON: How d' you like my surprise?
NAN: Not *too* much.
DON: *(taken aback)* Why not?
NAN: Well—for one thing—she's too old for you.
DON: *(grins)* I got news for you. I feel less like a kid every year.
NAN: Oh, Don! She's *much* too—well, experienced . . .
DON: That I like. *(pause)* Look—Nan. You're enjoying your life. Let me enjoy mine—huh?
She starts to speak further—thinks better of it.
Close shot of Brad and Christine.
CHRISTINE: *(looking offstage)* It's amazing—how much he reminds me of Frank Johnson—When Frank Johnson was young.
BRAD: I'm warning you. Lay off him. Let him alone.
CHRISTINE: *(sarcastically)* I suppose he's too clean and good for *me*?
BRAD: You bet he is.
CHRISTINE: Then all you have to do is tell him so. Tell him about my first big love affair—that you graduated from! *(mimicking)* "Why, Don, before Christine was seventeen years old—and I can prove it— I was *there* . . ." *(challenging)* You won't say a word to him. Not a word. You don't dare. *(mockingly)* And you bore me—Mr. Collins. But your brother-in-law doesn't. Odd—isn't it?
On his look we

DISSOLVE THROUGH TO INTERIOR TAXI—NIGHT
Don and Christine in embrace and kiss. She draws away slightly in his arms—studying him strangely.
CHRISTINE: You know, your—*family* wouldn't approve of this.
DON: *I* like it.
CHRISTINE: It—might even get to be a habit.
DON: I'd like that. *(pause)* I—wish you hadn't invited all those people to your apartment.
CHRISTINE: What people?

29

DON: Why—you told Brad and Nan a bunch was dropping in after the theatre.

CHRISTINE: They are. *(smiles)* Tomorrow night.

> *She sways to him and he responds. Their kiss is something new and wonderful to Don. Christine makes us wonder if it's altogether an act with her.*

FADE OUT

FADE IN

INTERIOR LANDING OUTSIDE CHRISTINE'S APARTMENT—NIGHT

> *Elevator doors open and Nixon and Arnold emerge. Music—from automatic-change phonograph—comes offstage from inside Christine's apartment.*

NIXON: *(to Arnold)* Wait out here.

> *Camera pans him to Christine's door. In pose of spectacled, rather shy "intellectual," Nixon enters. Music sound is louder—with voices and party laughter added—until door closes.*

INTERIOR CHRISTINE'S LIVING ROOM—NIGHT

> *Nixon drops hat on pile of coats and hats near door—continues into the room.*
>
> *Camera pulls back in front of him as he walks. It's a typical party of sophisticates. Men and women of various types and ages chat, drink, laugh—standing, seated, or lounging on floor. None notice Nixon—who seeks one person in particular.*
>
> *He passes a group around portable bar—the center of which is a well-dressed, bearded personage; the Professor.*
>
> *At length we're shooting over Nixon's shoulder—revealing that two couples dance to phonograph music. Camera centers on one couple—Christine and Don. They dance very close to each other—oblivious to others in the room.*
>
> *Christine and Don turn. Now for first time we see her face—and she sees Nixon. Almost at once, she disengages from Don's embrace. Of course, he doesn't know Nixon.*

30

CHRISTINE: Excuse me—darling.

As she moves from Don, Nixon turns and exits from shot. Christine speaks to a rather pretty girl—Evelyn.

CHRISTINE: *(continued)* Take care of Don 'til I get back.

EVELYN: Oh—glad to!

Evelyn starts Don toward portable bar. Christine exits following Nixon.

INTERIOR DARKROOM—NIGHT

Nixon enters—followed a second later by Christine. He hands her a roll of Leica film. During ensuing, Christine goes efficiently about business of preparing to develop this film. Nixon regards her thoughtfully.

CHRISTINE: *(as she works)* Couldn't this have waited?

NIXON: If it could—I wouldn't be here. *(brief pause)* Why is Johnson's brother-in-law here?

CHRISTINE: Because I invited him.

NIXON: Why?

CHRISTINE: *(sardonically)* Quote. One Party member should be able to indoctrinate a thousand non-Party members. Unquote.

NIXON: That depends on the purpose of the indoctrination. I suggest you stop seeing him after tonight.

CHRISTINE: *(tightening)* Is that an order?

Nixon shrugs. She gives him a look—snaps light out and starts developing film.

INTERIOR CHRISTINE'S LIVING ROOM—NIGHT

Close on Don and Evelyn. She has been holding forth to him— and he's doggedly unconvinced.

DON: I don't get it. I work. I get paid. Nobody can push me around. That makes this a pretty good country to live in—far as I'm concerned.

EVELYN: You don't think for yourself at all—do you, Mr. Lowry? *(calls offstage)* Oh—Professor . . .

Wider angle revealing Professor—who leaves a couple of people in background and moves to Evelyn and Don.

31

EVELYN: This young man has just been telling me that a democracy is the best of all possible worlds.
> *Professor comes to them. He's likeable—convincing. During ensuing, we get effect that both Professor and Evelyn talk down to Don—who is definitely out of his depth.*

PROFESSOR: He's quite right. Depending of course—on his definition of that much-misused word ... *democracy*. Your name, sir?

DON: Lowry. Don Lowry.

PROFESSOR: Mr. Lowry. Do you go to church, Mr. Lowry?

DON: Why—sure. Naturally.

PROFESSOR: Yet certain extremely intelligent philosophers call religion nothing but the opium of the masses.

DON: I've heard that and I don't believe it.

PROFESSOR: I see. Do you vote, Mr. Lowry?

DON: Sure. Naturally.

PROFESSOR: Yet a great many people believe the popular franchise as exercised in what you call a democracy is nothing more or less than a trick to fool the masses—once every four years—into the mistaken belief that they are controlling their destiny.

DON: That's—too much for *me* to figure out. Who fools *who*?

PROFESSOR: How do you decide who to vote for? By political conviction or ... ?

DON: I—don't know from politics. I just try to vote for the best man and let it go at that.

PROFESSOR: The best man for what?

DON: Why—for whatever he's running for.

EVELYN: *(amusedly contemptuous) Democracy in action!* The rugged young American individualist!

INTERIOR DARKROOM—NIGHT
> *We begin on Christine's hands rinsing a short piece of Leica film in tray—pull back as she hands film to Nixon, who slips it in viewer and studies it closely.*

CHRISTINE: *(in moment)* Important?

NIXON: *(continues studying film)* Very. As a matter of fact, it's what I've waited for—for the last eight months. *(still studies film while questioning)* How close is young Lowry to his brother-in-law?

CHRISTINE: *Very* close. Why?

NIXON: *(still studies film)* In that case—I've changed my mind about him. Continue with his indoctrination. I'll inform headquarters you personally guarantee he'll be delivered for use when and if he's needed.

Christine takes this with mingled reaction: pleasure about Don, puzzlement about Nixon's new purpose. She smiles, answering:

CHRISTINE: *(with slight mockery)* Why—that will be a very interesting assignment—that I will enjoy very much.

He gives her an unreadable side-look—hands strip of film to her.

NIXON: Destroy it.

She drops film in tray—takes bottle of chemical from shelf. Nixon exits. Christine pours acid on film. Fumes and vapor rise. She still smiles—about herself and Don.

INTERIOR LANDING OUTSIDE CHRISTINE'S APARTMENT—NIGHT

Nixon comes out—joining Arnold. Music and party sound are muffled offstage. Nixon starts to elevator with Arnold.

NIXON: *(as they move)* Call Charlie Dover for 11 o'clock. And right afterward—I'll want to see Frank Johnson. *(continues as they enter elevator)* The waterfront agit-prop cells are to be alerted for action beginning tomorrow morning . . .

During this, elevator door closes—cutting Nixon's orders.

INTERIOR CHRISTINE'S LIVING ROOM—NIGHT

Don is still being lectured by Professor. Evelyn listens—admiring the Professor, amused by Don. Several others have gathered to join in the fun.

PROFESSOR: . . . Young men, of course, believe the world is their oyster and they can open it with their bare hands. However, the truth is that many such venerable fables have long since been exploded— and not only by the atom bomb. Against the uninformed and un- disciplined system of majority rule, we set the modern system of a planned and managed State in which the people are guided and protected from their own errors of judgment and loyalty, for the greater good . . .

33

DON: *(interrupts)* You look like you'd done pretty well in your life. How'd you get your start?

PROFESSOR: As a matter of fact, I was brought up on a farm ...

During this, Christine enters in background—notes what's going on—moves to join Don.

DON: Looks to me like you're a pretty good ad for democracy—even if you don't like it.

EVELYN: He didn't say that!

DON: Then I need a new pair of ears!

CHRISTINE: *(appropriating Don)* End of argument. To be continued in our next ... *(starts Don away)* How about a breath of fresh air?

DON: *That* I could use.

Camera pans them toward door which opens on terrace.

EXTERIOR TERRACE OF CHRISTINE'S APARTMENT—NIGHT

Don and Christine come out and stand against balustrade. She watches Don—who stares out at the city's lights. After pause, she speaks lightly:

CHRISTINE: Sorry you came to my party?

DON: Why—no. I mean—not as far as *you're* concerned ...

CHRISTINE: But some of my guests bother you—don't they, darling?

DON: Kind of. They talk like I'm twelve years old and just out of kindergarten. Are they all friends of yours?

CHRISTINE: More or less.

DON: Do you agree with them?

CHRISTINE: Sometimes. Not always.

DON: Well—*I* don't.

CHRISTINE: Of course you don't—darling. Their ideas are all so new to you. But then—so am I.

She has deliberately injected a new note in their colloquy.

CHRISTINE: *(continued)* Just—keep an open mind, darling. You'll learn.

DON: *(responding)* Is that a—promise?

CHRISTINE: What do you think?

She sways into his arms. He holds her close.

34

CHRISTINE: *(continued)* I'm going to be very proud of you—Don—eventually.

It's Christine who kisses him, as we

DISSOLVE

INTERIOR PARTY ROOM—NIGHT
Nixon studies documents and gives orders to Charlie Dover—the Union man we met previously in Brad's office—who sits across table from Nixon.
Garth—the bodyguard—lounges silently in background.

NIXON: *(hands paper to Dover)* Those are the orders I received tonight—explicit, definite, *and to be carried out without fail.* The waterfront is to be tied up beginning May 18th for a period of at least 60 days. Therefore—no new contract between the Union and the owners is to be signed.

DOVER: *(protesting)* But—Collins and Jim Travis can practically close the deal on their own right now—and make it stick.

NIXON: I'll take care of—Collins. Your assignment is Travis.

DOVER: The Union's solid behind him.

NIXON: You know the techniques. Use them. Have your people make new demands at your meetings—that are bound to be refused by the owners. Use your key cells to block acceptance of any compromise. Start a whispering campaign. You'll be furnished with scripts for inflammatory speeches—attacks on the good-faith of the owners, on Travis as a company stooge . . .

During this, Nixon takes sheet of paper from folder.

NIXON: *(continued)* Here are some names of people still in process of indoctrination. You'll be told when, where and how you can use them.

He starts to hand paper to Dover—then thinks, and writes a new name at bottom of page.

INSERT TYPED LIST
We establish only what Nixon writes in long hand: Don Lowry.

Back to scene. Nixon hands list to Dover—who reacts when he sees Don's name.

DOVER: *(incredulously)* Collins' brother-in-law?

NIXON: *(oddly)* I'm informed he'll be ready for use when needed. He's not your problem. Make no contact with him at any time. *(dismissing curtly)* That's all for now.

Dover collects papers—exits. Nixon rises—starting to enter inner office.

NIXON: *(continued) (to Garth as he goes)* I'll see Johnson now.

INTERIOR INNER OFFICE—NIGHT

Nixon enters—unlocks steel filing cabinet, to which he returns folder. He rummages through other folders. During this business, we see Brad crossing Party room in background—followed by Garth. Brad enters. Garth stops in doorway.

Nixon keeps his back to Brad—continues search through folder during ensuing.

NIXON: Johnson—you are to see to it that no agreement is reached between your people and the Union.

Brad hasn't known what to expect. This is too much. He starts protest:

BRAD: Now—wait a minute . . .

NIXON: *(interrupts typically)* There must be a complete tieup of the waterfront beginning May 18th.

Brad takes this—moves a little closer during ensuing.

NIXON: *(continued) (still doesn't look at Brad)* Beginning immediately—in public, you will accuse Jim Travis and the Union of sabotaging negotiations. In private, you will inform Mr. Cornwall and the other owners that you recommend a reduction—not an increase—in wages . . .

BRAD: *(interrupts; protesting)* I'd never get away with it!

NIXON: *(half-wearily)* How many times do you think we've been through this before? We'll tell you what is to be done. How it's accomplished is *your* problem. *(continues with orders)* You will insist to the owners that now is the time for a showdown. You will refuse to discuss compromises with the Union—and if necessary you will refuse to submit to the Union any compromise proposed by the owners.

BRAD: If I try to pull anything like that I'll lose my job in a minute!

NIXON: *(still busy with files)* It's up to you to be clever enough to *keep* your job, Johnson. Otherwise you'll cease to have any value to the Party—and the Party will cease to have any reason for protecting you.

Closeup of Brad—realizing the crisis has come. After a moment:

NIXON'S VOICE: You're thinking—of course—that you don't need to obey your orders because we have no way to check up on you.

Brad reacts involuntarily—revealing this is just what he has been thinking.

NIXON'S VOICE: *(continued)* We don't *need* to check up on you. The Party judges by results. If the docks are still open May 18th—you will be held responsible . . . *(slight pause)* . . . And the following day you'll be under arrest for murder.

Brad can take no more. Killing Nixon with his hands is his only thought. He starts forward move—begins raising right hand to throw a punch. A gun fires from close offstage. Brad is creased by the shot—in flesh of upper right arm. This staggers him—stops his rush.

Another angle revealing that Garth fired at Brad—holds gun ready to fire again if need be. Brad—hurt although not gravely wounded—sways against desk. Nixon faces him directly for first time—removes spectacles while he says expressionlessly:

NIXON: He could have killed you just as easily. But the Party *doesn't want* you killed.

There's a moment's dead pause. Then Nixon says with commanding contempt:

NIXON: *(continued)* Go home, Johnson. And start carrying out your instructions first thing in the morning.

Brad shows furious helplessness. Blood begins to show through his ripped coat sleeve. Garth draws aside just a little. Slowly, Brad walks out.

DISSOLVE

INTERIOR COLLINS' LIVING ROOM—NIGHT

Brad lets himself in. By suggestion, he has found an "all-night doctor" somewhere—had his wound bandaged. His left arm is thrust in coat sleeve—but coat is loose over his right shoulder. His right arm—which pains him considerably—hangs limp at his side.

Going to sideboard, Brad gets bottle and glass—pours with left hand—drinks.

NAN'S VOICE: Brad?

He turns—startled, endeavoring to stand so that his wound won't be noticed.

We deliver Nan on stairs. She wears night-dress—has just risen from sleep.

NAN: You were gone so long. I kept calling your office and couldn't get an answer.

BRAD: *(best he can do)* I—had to go to a meeting.

NAN: Is everything all right?

BRAD: Sure. Of course. *(voice is edged)* Go on back to bed, Nan.

But she comes the rest of the way to him.

NAN: Everything's *not* all right.

He turns from her—pours another drink—gulps it.

NAN: *(continued) (close to him)* Brad—don't you want to—talk about it? It—might help.

BRAD: *(turns on her—harshly)* Talk about *what*? I asked you to go back to bed. *(she doesn't move)* Nan—I've got to think some things out—make plans . . .

As he speaks, she notes how his coat is slung over bandaged arm. Before he realizes, she moves—pushes the coat aside—sees the blood-stained bandage, his shirt cut away, and reacts tensely:

NAN: Brad! You're hurt!

Desperate—forced at all costs to cover the truth—he bursts out at her angrily:

BRAD: *(mimicking)* "Brad! You're hurt!" All right—I'm hurt. Yes. Somebody took a shot at me down at the docks. That's *my* business—and I'll take care of it. Now go on back to bed!

Instead, she starts move to telephone. He stops her:

38

BRAD: *(continued)* What do you think *you're* going to do? Call the police, I suppose?

NAN: *(bewildered)* Why—yes ...

BRAD: *(left hand grips her arm cruelly)* I said *I'll* take care of it. Worry about your home. Let *me* worry about the rest of it. Now go on back to bed and let me alone!

She draws back—staring at him unbelievingly.

NAN: Brad ...

He swings to sideboard—pours another drink.

BRAD: *(over shoulder)* You heard me! Go on!

Nothing like this has happened between them before. She shows shock and dismay. Hesitantly, she turns—goes back up the stairs. In a moment, bedroom door closes behind her. Now at last Brad dares to drop his pose. He gulps drink—sinks down in chair. Camera moves in on Brad—who suddenly bows his head in hands.

FADE OUT

FADE IN

MONTAGE—STOCK SHOTS SAN FRANCISCO SHIPPING.

OUT OF WHICH COME:

NEWSPAPER HEADLINE:
WATERFRONT WAGE TALKS START

IMPRESSION SHOT OF MEETING IN BRAD'S OFFICE
Brad is speaking—curtly, almost belligerently.

BIG HEAD OF DOVER
angrily interrupting.

BIG HEAD OF TRAVIS

trying to shut him up.

NEWSPAPER HEADLINE:
WATERFRONT WAGE PARLEY STRIKES SURPRISE SNAG

BIG HEAD OF NIXON
reading this newspaper satisfiedly.

IMPRESSION SHOT OF A SUBSEQUENT MEETING
Travis is now speaking.

BIG HEAD OF BRAD
suddenly interrupting him.

BIG HEAD OF TRAVIS
surprised reaction to what he says.

BIG HEAD OF DOVER
pleasantly satisfied with the way things are going.

IMPRESSION SHOT OF NEGOTIATORS
All pretty glum, leaving a building. (Brad is not present.) Reporters try to grab them; only Charlie Dover is willing to talk, which he does with a show of anger.

NEWSPAPER HEADLINE:
STALEMATE FEARED IN WATERFRONT WAGE TALKS

SHOT OF DON AND CHRISTINE
discussing this newspaper. She talks—and Don looks convinced.

IMPRESSION SHOT OF MEETING OF UNION LEADERS
Charlie Dover is giving a violent harangue.

IMPRESSION SHOT IN CORNER OF A RESTAURANT
Brad is arguing with Cornwall.

POSTER
Announcing Union Mass Meeting.

IMPRESSION OF UNION MEETING
Travis, as chairman, finishes speaking and recognizes a speaker.

CLOSE SHOT OF DON
as he stands up to speak, violently and passionately.

NEWSPAPER HEADLINE:
OWNER'S ATTITUDE ASSAILED BY LABOR SPOKESMEN

CLOSE SHOT ON JIM TRAVIS
looking surprised.

CLOSE SHOT OF DOVER
delighted.

IMPRESSION OF MEETING OF SHIPOWNERS
Brad—newspaper in his hand—is violently stirring up the meeting.

BIG HEAD OF CORNWALL
not altogether convinced—but giving in—he nods.

NEWSPAPER HEADLINE:
WATERFRONT NEGOTIATIONS BROKEN OFF

BIG HEAD OF NIXON
satisfied with results of his scheme.

BIG HEAD OF BRAD
his face set and grim—heavy with guilt.

FADE OUT

FADE IN

INTERIOR CHRISTINE'S LIVING ROOM—NIGHT

Christine enters from bedroom and crosses to sofa on which is a quite small, almost-packed bag. She brings a couple of articles as last-minute additions. It's obvious her temper is not good.

As the camera pans over, we see Nixon seated—making some notes on pad. He wears his spectacles—through which he studies her.

NIXON: Is that all you're taking?

CHRISTINE: I'll only be gone a couple of days.

NIXON: You'll be away a week. Perhaps much longer.

She reacts.

CHRISTINE: *(resentfully)* You keep forgetting I get paid to work for the magazine—which is a very valuable front. They know how long the Seattle assignment will take.

NIXON: You'll have to convince them you need more time.

He hands her notes he has been writing.

NIXON: *(continued)* Make these contacts and transmit these instructions.

She scans notes—tightens.

CHRISTINE: Any messenger-boy could take care of this.

NIXON: I want *you* to take care of it. *(pause)* You've finished the indoctrination of young Lowry satisfactorily. Now I think for your own good you'd better be out of sight of him long enough to get your emotions under control—before they get you in serious trouble.

CHRISTINE: *(defiantly)* I'll worry about my private life.

NIXON: You *have* no private life. *(deliberately)* You started out in spite—and pretended Party purposes only to hide your real motives. But now you've begun to think you're in love with the young man—which is ridiculous. As a result, you're beginning to forget your position and mine—which is dangerous.

He rises and prepares to exit.

NIXON: *(continued)* I'll hope that while you're in Seattle you'll come to your senses. Otherwise . . .

CHRISTINE: Otherwise what?

NIXON: The Party will decide that.

He walks out. She stands raging. Suddenly, she gets hat and coat—gives herself one last look in mirror—picks up her bag—is exiting as we

DISSOLVE

INTERIOR AIRPORT—NIGHT
Don—in work-clothes—moves back and forth restlessly in alcove of waiting-room. He consults wrist-watch—looks offstage impatiently—nervously lights a cigarette.
ANNOUNCER'S VOICE: Flight 671 for Portland and Seattle—now loading at Gate 4.
Don reacts to this—looks at watch again—then at last sees Christine approaching hurriedly. Almost hysterical, no longer poised and sophisticated, she runs into his arms—clings to him, sobbing.
DON: *(taken aback)* Hey—hey, Chris! What *is* this? *(tips her chin up)* You never acted like *this* before.
CHRISTINE: *(unsteadily)* I—never *felt* like this before. *(again clings)* Oh—Don—*hold* me!
DON: A pleasure! *(in moment)* You know—after all—you're not going to Siberia or something. Just to Seattle. And only for a couple of days.
ANNOUNCER'S VOICE: Flight 671 for Portland and Seattle—now loading at Gate 4. All aboard, please.
CHRISTINE: *(reacting)* That's my 'plane.
DON: *(doesn't release her)* Don't take it.
CHRISTINE: I have to.
DON: No, you don't. Quit your job.
CHRISTINE: *(with double meaning)* I—*can't* quit.
DON: Sure you can. Quit and marry me.
She takes this with stunned realization.
CHRISTINE: Don—do you really *want* to *marry* me?
DON: I never thought of it 'til just now. But it's a fine idea. Solves everything.
CHRISTINE: No questions—no doubts—just ... You *do* love me—don't you?
DON: You or nobody, Chris.
CHRISTINE: And I—I love *you*. It's silly—ridiculous—impossible—wrong—and I don't care. *I don't care. (voice breaking)* Oh, Don—Don ...

Again, she clings. They kiss passionately.
FLIGHT ANNOUNCER'S VOICE: Miss Christine Norman—Miss Christine Norman—Flight 671 is being held for you—please go to Gate 4 immediately.
Desperately, she frees herself from Don's arms.
DON: *(amazed)* Hey—Chris . . .
She runs from him—disappearing.
Close shot on Don watching her go—tempted to follow—then beginning to grin. She'll be back in a few days. He can wait. He starts off.

INTERIOR AIRPORT 'PHONE BOOTH—NIGHT
Don completes dialing of a number—while roaring sound comes offstage, of airplane taxiing past outside along runway.
Camera is outside the booth. Because of sound, we don't hear what Don says at beginning on 'phone.
His eyes follow 'plane movement offstage as he speaks. Sound fades. Now we hear:
DON: *(on 'phone)* I said—married. *(pause)* You know. Like you and Brad and all the best people. *(answering query on 'phone)* Why—sure it's Christine. Who else? And why not?

INTERIOR COLLINS' KITCHEN—NIGHT
Shot is over Nan—who speaks on kitchen extension 'phone in foreground. She wears hostess gown.
In background Brad "breaks" ice cubes from refrigerator tray— dumps cubes in ice bucket. He wears dressing gown over shirt and trousers. He pays little heed to Nan's talk.
NAN: *(crisply on 'phone)* I can think of a *lot* of reasons why not—and so could *you*—if you'd stop and think straight for a minute. *(answers Don's protest over 'phone)* No—I *don't* approve. Not at all. *(against Don's further argument)* We'll talk about it some other time. Not tonight.
She hangs up—just as Brad comes to her carrying ice bucket on tray.
BRAD: What was that all about?
NAN: *(covering)* Oh—just Don with another one of his wild ideas.

BRAD: *(not too interested)* Anything serious?

NAN: It had better *not* be.

Brad starts to inquire further. She stops him with:

NAN: *(continued)* After all—you married *me*—not my family.

Brad's look says he agrees with this. They exit.

INTERIOR LOBBY OF COLLINS' APARTMENT—NIGHT

They're crossing to enter living room when door buzzer sound surprises both.

Brad—his hands full—proceeds offstage. Nan moves to open door. She faces Jim Travis.

Nan is surprised but pleased. Jim is understandably diffident.

NAN: Why—Jim—it's about time you came to see us.

JIM: Well—under the circumstances—I figured—better if I didn't bother you and Brad. But something's come up—pretty important—that I have to talk to Brad about.

She helps Jim with his hat and coat—as Brad enters from living room. She can't help noticing Brad's not as pleased to see Jim as she hoped he'd be.

BRAD: *(as he enters)* Oh—hello, Jim.

JIM: Sorry to bust in on you so late—but I just came from a meeting of the Policy Committee.

BRAD: Oh. Well—come on in.

He turns to re-enter living room. Jim and Nan follow.

INTERIOR COLLINS' LIVING ROOM—NIGHT

Brad moves to sideboard—offers over shoulder:

BRAD: How about a drink?

JIM: Later—maybe.

Brad pours highballs for himself and Nan. She accepts hers but doesn't drink.

BRAD: What's on your mind?

JIM: Well—kind of a forlorn hope. Don't know if it'll do any good—but I thought I'd come and try it on you, anyhow.

BRAD: Try what?

JIM: In spite of the hotheads, the boys authorized me to make one more pitch at reopening negotiations.

45

BRAD: On what basis?

JIM: If you'll bring your people back for another talk—I'll bring mine.

BRAD: Can't do it, Jim.

JIM: But—why not?

BRAD: Your demands are so far out of line that it'd be a waste of time.

Nan reacts to this curt finality. So does Jim.

JIM: Now—wait a minute. There's right and wrong on both sides. Why can't we both admit it—and go on from there?

Brad affects sardonic ease—to mask his actual problem.

BRAD: You know, Jim—I don't have to stand still for any cross-examinations.

JIM: No—you don't. *(shrugs grimly)* Well—I said it was a forlorn hope.

He's about to go, when Nan speaks.

NAN: Brad—may I ask a question?

BRAD: *(pours himself a fresh drink)* What?

NAN: Why *won't* you reopen negotiations? I know you don't want a lot of men put out of work—some of them your old friends ...

BRAD: *(interrupts harshly)* Nan—do you mind?

It's like a slap in her face. Jim reacts. Nan—puzzled and hurt—carries it off as well as she can.

NAN: I'm—sorry. I'll—get back to my own department.

On this, she turns and exits. Jim looks after her. Brad turns away. Close shot on Jim. Brad's face is out of camera. Jim moves to inspect Brad's cargo-hook, Union button—and especially the stevedore-days photos displayed on wall.

JIM: *(after pause)* You were quite a guy, in those days. *(looks at Brad)* Still quite a guy—until just lately.

During this, Brad turns to face him. He has his mask on.

JIM: *(continued)* What's come over you, Brad? What's wrong with you?

Brad tightens—uses anger as his shield.

BRAD: Nothing's wrong with me. Not a thing.

Deliberately, he poises decanter above glass.

46

BRAD: *(continued)* Well—it's bedtime for working people. *(indicates)* How about one for the road?
JIM: I'll do without it.
Brad waits for him to go. But Jim delays briefly.
JIM: *(continued)* One thing before I go. I'll give it to you straight. I walked in here with a fair proposition. I'm walking out turned down for no good reason . . .
Brad's anger rises—because he knows Jim's anger is justified.
JIM: *(continued)* All right. I want to put this on record. If there's a waterfront tieup—you, not the Union, will be responsible. We tried. You *won't* try. *(turns to exit)* Good night, Brad.
He exits toward lobby.
Close on Brad. Seething—trapped—he punches fist in palm of hand. Display on wall behind him is significant.

INTERIOR LOBBY OF COLLINS' APARTMENT—NIGHT
Jim enters—is getting his hat and coat when Nan enters from kitchen.
NAN: *(helping him with coat)* I'm—sorry, Jim.
JIM: So am I, Nan. *(after pause)* If things had turned out a little different, I had it in mind to bring up something—kind of personal.
NAN: What, Jim?
JIM: Well—about Don.
NAN: What?
JIM: *(reluctantly)* I can't figure the way he's acting lately.
NAN: Neither can I. *(as the big sister)* He—called up a while ago announcing he's getting married.
JIM: What's wrong with that?
NAN: The woman he wants to marry. Christine Norman.
JIM: *(echoes; reacting)* Christine Norman? Well! That explains a lot. I couldn't figure him—shooting his mouth off at the meetings— preaching the Commie line word for word. Makes sense, now—if *she's* got her hooks in him.
What Jim is opening up is new and startling to Nan.
BRAD'S VOICE: Jim—if you don't mind—Nan and I'll keep our family affairs in the family.

47

Both turn—startled.
Another angle revealing Brad—who has just entered from living room.

NAN: But—Brad—I want to hear what Jim knows about Christine Norman.

BRAD: Well—what *do* you know, Jim?

JIM: The talk's around that she's at least a fellow-traveler—and probably a practicing Commie.

BRAD: *(rather amusedly)* That's what the Law calls information and belief—not evidence. Trouble with you boys, Jim—you've got Commies on the brain. Anybody doesn't agree with you—he's a Commie. The old smear technique. And kind of dangerous—I've heard—when you can't prove it.

JIM: *(heatedly)* If I could prove what I suspect, there's a dozen smart troublemakers in the Union I'd be after right now.

BRAD: *(smiling)* Then I tell you what you do, Jim. You go chase the Commies in your Union and let Nan and me worry about Don. *(pause; curtly)* Goodnight, Jim!

Jim hesitates—looks to Nan—exits.
Close on Nan. She has much to wonder about.

BRAD'S VOICE: Honey—there's a nightcap in here with your name on it.

Nan hesitates. She smiles, starts into living room as we

DISSOLVE

INTERIOR COLLINS' BEDROOM—NIGHT
Nan in night-dress and robe lies on her bed. She's deep in unhappy thought.
From bathroom in background of shot we hear sound of Brad brushing his teeth. As sound stops, Nan calls:

NAN: Brad.

BRAD'S VOICE: What, honey?

NAN: Wouldn't it be awful if Jim was right about Christine?

Brad—in silk pajamas and dressing-gown—enters from bathroom. He attempts casual dismissal:

BRAD: Not a chance. Wouldn't *she* be an idiot to get mixed up with the Commies? The highest paid woman in her racket?
He goes to Nan's dressing table—picks up bottle of cologne.
BRAD: *(continued)* Is this stuff any good?
NAN: *(half-smiles)* It ought to be. You bought it for me.
He grins at her—dabs cologne on hands, then on face and neck.
NAN: *(continued) (after pause)* Jim's not the kind to accuse people without reason.
Brad comes and sits on bed beside her.
BRAD: Jim's the guy that didn't get to marry you. I'm the guy that did.
She looks in his eyes searchingly.
BRAD: *(continued)* Honey. This is home. This is us. Let's let the rest of the world roll by—for a while, anyhow.
She begins to yield. He proceeds with campaign:
BRAD: *(continued)* Do you realize this is another anniversary? Three months ago tonight.
He starts to play with her ear.
BRAD: *(continued)* Remind me to tell you some time what nice ears you have.
She puts her hand on his. He kisses her hand—is about to kiss her lips.
NAN: *(suddenly)* Brad—I've got to know!
BRAD: Know what?
NAN: Was Christine a Communist when you—knew her?
BRAD: *(grins; evading)* Honey—I never ask a lady about her politics.
He takes her face between his hands.
BRAD: *(continued)* Now can we start thinking about us?
He presses her close.
Big closeup of Nan—as Brad kisses her. Despite his kiss, she's still unconvinced.

FADE OUT

FADE IN

EXTERIOR SAN FRANCISCO WATERFRONT—

49

DAY (STOCK)

DISSOLVE THROUGH TO CHECKER'S HUT AND PIER (STUDIO)—DAY
On process plate, a freighter is loading. Throughout ensuing scene, we have background movement of cranes, etc. freight being hoisted aboard.
Don in stevedore clothes, cargo-hook thrust through belt—gets signatures on manifests clipped to board, from a cargo mate (call him Cahill).

CAHILL: *(accepting clip-board)* May not see you again for a while—hah?

DON: Maybe not.

CAHILL: Ask *me*—you guys are nuts—and so are the owners—tyin' things up when you could get together easy if you wanted to.

DON: I didn't ask you. Get it?
During this, Jim Travis enters. Don is aware of Jim—but is about to exit without saying anything when Jim speaks.

JIM: Don.

DON: *(coldly)* What?

JIM: I want to have a talk with you.

DON: What's the matter? Sore because I said a few things you didn't like at the meetings? It's a free country—in case you hadn't heard.

JIM: Sure is.

DON: Well, then—what about it?
Close shot on Jim and Don. Jim takes his time—lounges on cargo-bale, lights pipe, puffs, studies Don.

JIM: Don, part of my job as I see it is to keep Commie influence out of the Union.

DON: I'm no Commie and you know it!

JIM: I said "Commie influence."

DON: *(challengingly)* Meaning *what?*

JIM: Do you know how the Commies operate?

DON: No—I don't. And I'm not interested.

JIM: You ought to be. Because you're in with them up to your neck.

DON: I think you're out of your mind.

JIM: *(rising unhurriedly)* It's the truth, Don. Even if you don't know it. If people like you weren't so ignorant—the Commies wouldn't be so dangerous.

DON: Look—if I want to learn about politics, I'll go read a good book.

JIM: I'm not talking politics. I'm talking about Commies. They're not a Party of the masses. They don't want the masses. They're a Party of the select few—who think they can impose on the masses their idea of what's good for them.

DON: *(interrupts)* You ought to go on a lecture tour. "The Truth About Communism—Free-Will Offerings Taken Up After the Meeting!"

JIM: Don—I wouldn't be lecturing *you* if I didn't think a lot of you and your family. There's one thing I *know*—that it's time you found out. Because they *are* a Party of the few out to boss the world—every Commie has to be an active conspirator—recruit stooges—who usually don't even know they're being used. Well-meaning liberals— the underprivileged—the unemployed—and lovesick kids like *you*.

Closeup of Don—looking at Jim in furious amazement.

JIM'S VOICE: Why've *you* been spouting the Commie line word for word? One reason—only one. Because this woman you're crazy about has been using you—*the way she's used plenty of others before you* . . .

Don lunges—throwing a wild punch at Jim.

Close shot on Jim and Don. Jim blocks Don's punch expertly— grips his wrists. Stronger than Don, he holds him while he continues grimly:

JIM: What do I have to do—*beat* some sense into you? If you've got guts enough—go ask her. Unless you're afraid of what you'll find out.

Almost contemptuously, he shoves Don away—turns and exits. Don starts instinctive move to go after him—then stops. Close shot on Don—for his furious reaction. He's turning out of camera as we

DISSOLVE

INTERIOR CHRISTINE'S LIVING ROOM—DAY

Christine enters—carrying some small bag we saw before.
As camera pans her across the room, Don's head and shoulders
come into foreground of the shot. He has changed to street clothes.
He watches in silence until Christine realizes his presence. She
turns—starts to him gladly.

CHRISTINE: Why—Don—darling!

He doesn't speak or move.

CHRISTINE: *(continued)* Why weren't you at the airport?

DON: *(flat-voiced)* I thought we could talk better here.

CHRISTINE: Is there something wrong?

DON: That's what I want to find out—And—just don't lie to me.
Christine can't help realizing something has happened. She
abandons lightness—speaks with deep sincerity:

CHRISTINE: Don—I couldn't lie to you if I wanted to—and I don't
want to, ever as long as I live. You see—I really love you, Don. I
never meant to—but I do.

DON: Me or the Commy Party?

Now she knows what it's about.

DON: *(continued)* I've been told you're a Commy agent.
Her thinking is "Has Brad talked?" She questions—denying
nothing:

CHRISTINE: Who told you that?

DON: Jim Travis.

CHRISTINE: Oh—the Union man. *(now she's not quite so concerned)*
What did he say? I—want you to tell me exactly, Don.

DON: He said you're a Commy—that you've been using me—the
way you've used plenty of others before me.

CHRISTINE: Oh. I see.
Momentarily, she turns out of camera—makes business of re-
moving hat and coat, while planning just what she'll say. After
pause, Don demands:

DON: Well—what about it?

She turns to him—is outwardly composed.

CHRISTINE: I'm sorry it turned out this way. I knew I should tell you
myself. That's one of the reasons why I came back sooner than I was
supposed to.

DON: Then you—you really *are* ...

CHRISTINE: I'm a Party member—yes. I *have* been for years. Yes, Don.

He stares at her.

CHRISTINE: *(continued)* Oh, Don—what's politics got to do with you and me?

DON: Plenty! You've just made a sucker out of me—a Commy stooge ... You're not in love with me. You never *were* ...

CHRISTINE: *(interrupts; anger rising)* Don—that's not true!

DON: Stop lying! You've done enough of that!

Suddenly, he grabs her arms—hurting her.

DON: *(continued)* Why, I ought to ...

CHRISTINE: Listen to me, Don. I love you. I didn't at first. I used you—yes. That was my job. And I never *wanted* to fall in love with you. I knew it was a mistake and both of us might suffer for it. But I couldn't help myself. I love you, Don ... and *that's all that ought to matter!*

DON: *(releases her with bitter contempt)* A Commy agent—working for the Party ...

CHRISTINE: And what's wrong with that? I said you had a lot to learn. Let me tell you something, Don. There are a lot of fine things about Communism. A lot of fine people in the Party.

DON: *Name one!*

She stares at him strangely—in silence for a moment. Fear of losing him—emotional instability—anger—prompt her decision:

CHRISTINE: *(rather quietly)* I can do that, Don. I guess it's time I did. It'll be a shock to you. But maybe that's what you need.

As she speaks, she moves to desk—unlocks drawer—takes out Brad's dossier—and climactically offers this toward Don.

CHRISTINE: *(continued)* Look at it.

Don accepts dossier—reacts to what he sees.

INSERT OF *DOSSIER*

in Don's hands. He turns photostats and photos—comes finally to photo of Brad and Christine as lovers.

CHRISTINE'S VOICE: *(in rising tirade)* If being a Party member makes me some kind of a social leper—I'm not the only one! Oh, no! Maybe it's possible for people to be Communists and still be human beings, too! Maybe it is—even if you don't believe it!

Back to scene. Don stands stunned—wordless, sickened, rooted.

CHRISTINE: *(right on; all restraint or caution forgotten)* Does that make any difference? *Does* it, Don? *Answer* me, Don! What do you think *now* about . . .

Suddenly, she breaks off—staring at someone offstage.

Another angle over Christine—delivering Nixon in doorway. He has just entered—takes in the whole situation—closes door and advances silently. Christine and Don are motionless.

NIXON: *(reaching them; to Christine)* You were under orders to stay in Seattle until you heard from me.

She doesn't answer—can't. Nixon takes dossier *from Don's hands.*

NIXON: *(continued)* Mr. Lowry—you will forget you ever saw this.

DON: *(to Christine)* Who's he? One of your Commy pals?

NIXON: *(gives Christine no chance to answer)* I'm about to become your very good friend. That is—I'm going to give you some good advice—for which you'll thank me later. *(typically)* You are to forget that Bradley Collins is also Frank Johnson. You are not to see Miss Norman again. You will go about your business—and keep your mouth shut. Otherwise—your brother-in-law will be in very serious trouble.

DON: *(savagely)* That'll be just too bad—won't it?

He turns to leave. Nixon catches his arm.

NIXON: You had better listen to me . . .

Don smashes fist to Nixon's face. He reels backward—but doesn't go down. Don exits—slamming door.

Close shot on Nixon and Christine. Nixon produces snowy handkerchief—dabs fastidiously at bleeding mouth.

NIXON: *(after pause)* You were warned. *(another pause)* If the shipowners—the Union—the newspapers—or the public—learn the truth about Frank Johnson from him . . . Johnson will cease to be of any value. Then I will be held responsible. *I*—not *you.*

CHRISTINE: He'll—only go to Brad. Brad will make him keep quiet.

54

NIXON: We won't depend on Brad—as you call him.

He dabs again at bleeding lip—as he prepares to leave.

CHRISTINE: What are you going to do?

NIXON: *(gives her a contemptuous look; curtly)* You will stay in this apartment. You will not communicate with anyone.

Fastidiously, he drops stained handkerchief in wastebasket. He exits.

Close shot on Christine—staring after Nixon. She knows Don's deadly danger—and her own.

DISSOLVE THROUGH TO INTERIOR INNER OFFICE— DAY

Closeup of Don's dossier being taken from files—featuring photo of Don clipped from Christine's magazine layout.

ARNOLD'S VOICE: *(speaking on 'phone)* Oh—I see. Yes, Mr. Nixon. Right away. I'll take care of it.

Close shot on Arnold—talking on 'phone. He concludes:

ARNOLD: *(on 'phone)* Yes, Mr. Nixon.

He hangs up—puts dossier in pocket—is hurrying out as we

DISSOLVE

EXTERIOR SHOOTING GALLERY—DAY—(PROCESS)

At opening of shot, we do not see the gallery—but get a vista of beach, Ferris-wheel turning, roller-coaster.

Arnold emerges from crowd. As he moves into camera, we hear rifle-shots—bongg! of bullets hitting metal targets.

As camera pans with Arnold, we deliver the shooting-gallery— and Bailey doing a spiel to a few customers.

Arnold waits with back to camera—for Bailey to notice him. In moment, Bailey sees him. He turns to Jeb—a dull-witted water- front bum, who hangs around the gallery, loading guns, setting up the targets, and doing odd jobs.

BAILEY: Take over 'til I get back. And keep your mitts out of the till or I'll saw 'em off.

To Bailey, this threat is humour. He leaves booth—giving a look at Arnold as he goes.

55

Arnold follows him out of picture.

BAILEY: *(continued) (as they exit)* Well—what's the deal this time . . . ?

DISSOLVE

INTERIOR BRAD'S OUTER OFFICE—NIGHT
Brad enters—wearing hat and coat.

SECRETARY: Oh—Mr. Collins! You just missed Mr. Lowry. He was here waiting for a long while. He seemed very upset about something.
She is interrupted by ringing of 'phone.

SECRETARY: *(continued) (answering)* Mr. Collins' office. Oh—just a moment. *(covers receiver)* It's a Miss Norman. She's called several times.

BRAD: I'm not in. Won't be—any time she calls.

SECRETARY: *(on 'phone)* I'm *sorry,* Miss Norman.

INTERIOR CHRISTINE'S LIVING ROOM—NIGHT
She argues over 'phone with Brad's secretary.

CHRISTINE: But surely you know where to reach him. Can't you understand—I *must* talk to him. Ohh . . . !
She slams receiver up—stares again at nothing—then begins to dial another number.

EXTERIOR STREET OUTSIDE COLLINS' APARTMENT—
NIGHT
Convertible with top down drives down the street. As it stops near camera, we see the driver is Don.
A moment later a battered old black sedan drives up and stops a little behind.
The driver of the black sedan. It is Bailey—watching Don. Beside him is Arnold—who indicates toward Don as he gets out of car. Arnold walks away briskly—back the way he came.
Don, from Bailey's angle. Before getting out of his car, Don takes out a pack of cigarettes, puts one in his mouth, fumbles for a match.
Close shot of Bailey watching and waiting.

56

INTERIOR COLLINS' LIVING ROOM—NIGHT
This shot is taken through an open window and shows Nan on the telephone. She wears houserobe.
NAN: *(puzzled but forceful)* Look—Christine—you can't just call up and say "Don's in danger" and let it go at that. *What* danger? What have you gotten Don mixed up in?

EXTERIOR STREET OUTSIDE COLLINS' APARTMENT—NIGHT
Don—having lit his cigarette—gets out of his car and starts across street.
Flash of Bailey as he lets in clutch and car leaps forward.
Flash of Don. He turns at sound of oncoming car.
Flash of sedan as it bears down on Don.
Flash of Don. He tries to leap to safety on sidewalk.
Close shot of Bailey. He swings wheel—driving onto sidewalk to hit Don.

INTERIOR COLLINS' LIVING ROOM—NIGHT
There's a terrific car-crash sound from street. Nan drops 'phone—runs to the window—reacts in horror.

EXTERIOR STREET OUTSIDE COLLINS' APARTMENT—NIGHT
What Nan sees: Death car swerving back onto street—and a crumpled body lying half on sidewalk, half in street.
The camera zooms down to the body of Don.

DISSOLVE

INTERIOR COLLINS' LIVING ROOM—NIGHT
Close on Nan. She's tearless—frozen by shock—holding something back. She still wears houserobe.
POLICEMAN'S VOICE: I'm afraid that's about it, Mr. Collins. Hit-run driver—witnesses weren't close enough to get the license number—not much chance the driver'll be caught.
During this, we go to

Another angle including Brad and a brisk, rather young Police Traffic Officer. Brad's eyes are on Nan.

POLICEMAN: I'll have to ask you to come over to the Traffic Bureau—Mr. Collins—details, you know ...

BRAD: Is it absolutely necessary to go through all that tonight?

POLICEMAN: Afraid so, Mr. Collins.

BRAD: All right. I'll be with you in a minute.

Policeman nods understandingly—returns notebook to pocket—starts out.

POLICEMAN: 'Night, Mrs. Collins. Sure am sorry.

Nan doesn't answer—hardly hears him—is staring strangely at Brad.

NAN: *(when Policeman is gone; oddly quiet)* Brad—it wasn't an accident.

BRAD: What else could it be?

NAN: *(as before)* Christine Norman knew it was going to happen. She was on the telephone telling me Don was in danger—when I heard the crash and ran to the window and ...

She breaks—turns from him—can't continue for moment.

BRAD: Nan—for all *we* know—Christine and Don had a row—maybe he was so worked up he wasn't watching—walked right out in front of the car ...

NAN: *(turns to him; strangely)* I *wondered* what you'd say. Do you really believe that?

BRAD: I certainly don't believe Don was murdered. What reason would anybody have for killing him?

NAN: The police could find out. They could force her to tell them what she wouldn't tell *me*.

Idea of telling the police is startling to Brad—must be headed off.

BRAD: *(almost desperately)* Nan—think a minute. If you say anything to the police about her call—it will mean newspaper scandal—linking Don with Christine—doing nobody any good.

NAN: Then call *her.*

BRAD: What?

NAN: I've never asked how close you were in the past. I don't want to know. But you've got to make her tell you how she knew Don was going to be killed. Call her.

58

BRAD: No.

NAN: Then *I will!*

She moves to 'phone. He stops her forcibly.

BRAD: No, Nan!

NAN: Are you *afraid* to let me call her? Is that it, Brad? Is that what's wrong with you?

BRAD: Nan—listen . . .

NAN: *(right on)* What are you protecting? Don's reputation? Or Christine? *Or yourself?*

BRAD: Nan—I've had about enough of this!

NAN: And so have I! I married you—knowing very little about you. But I trusted you. Many things have puzzled me—but I've gone on trusting you. But right now—I *don't.*

Closeup of Brad. Here is the showdown—and he must meet it somehow.

NAN's VOICE: I had a brother I loved. He's dead. I want to know who killed him—and why. *And I'm going to find out.*

Close shot on Nan over Brad. He meets her challenge with sudden sincerity.

BRAD: Nan—what kind of a man do you think I am? *(hands on her arms)* Do you think I'm low enough—to back away from a show-down—if Don's death *was* anything but an accident? *(half-shakes her—not cruelly)* Nan—you know me better than that. *Don't* you?

She stares at him—not entirely convinced. Door-buzzer sound comes offstage.

BRAD: *(continued)* I can't keep that cop waiting. But I'll be back in a little while. Then we'll figure things out the best we can. *(gently compelling)* Go on upstairs now and try to rest. *Will* you?

She turns away wordlessly—moves slowly upstairs.

We hold with Brad watching, until she enters bedroom and closes door. At last he turns into camera. He's grim—tortured—not at all triumphant. Door-buzzer sounds again, imperatively this time. Brad scowls—starts out to join Policeman as we

DISSOLVE

INTERIOR PARTY ROOM INNER OFFICE—NIGHT

We start with closeup of Nixon's hands—counting ten large bills (by suggestion, ten $100 notes) on desk.

NIXON'S VOICE: Nine hundred—a thousand.

During this, camera pulls back—revealing Nixon—then Bailey, then Arnold and Garth (the bodyguard who as usual stands in background). Arnold is shaken by what has recently transpired. Bailey is swaggering—smug—greedy.

BAILEY: I figure I'm entitled to somethin' extra. Nice neat job—took kind of a big chance puttin' it over.

NIXON: *(with icy contempt)* You'll take what you get and be satisfied.

Bailey starts to protest further—subsides under Nixon's cold gaze.

BAILEY: Okay—okay.

'Phone rings. Arnold answers:

ARNOLD: *J. T. Arnold Import-Export. (reacts)* Oh, Miss Norman.

He looks inquiry at Nixon—who shakes head.

ARNOLD: *(continued) (over 'phone)* He's not here. *(with asperity)* I haven't the slightest idea when he'll be in or where you could contact him.

He hangs up—cutting sound of Christine's voice over 'phone.

INTERIOR CHRISTINE'S LIVING ROOM—NIGHT

She turns from 'phone—paces with constantly mounting nervousness. She stops—staring at Don's framed photograph on desk.

DISSOLVE

INTERIOR COLLINS' LIVING ROOM—NIGHT

Brad enters—returning from Traffic Bureau. Lights are on as when he left. Nan isn't seen.

Brad makes us feel he suffers from guilt because of Don's death. An innately decent man, he knows what he must do in common decency. But it's hard to begin.

Much like Christine—and with equivalent desperation—he walks back and forth, striking balled fist in palm of hand. At

60

length—suddenly—he reaches final decision. At once, he starts up stairs to bedroom.

INTERIOR COLLINS' BEDROOM—NIGHT
Brad enters—calling:

BRAD: Nan!

Camera pans from his viewpoint. Nan is gone. Houserobe tossed aside on bed is eloquent. He turns—hurrying back down stairs.

INTERIOR CHRISTINE'S LIVING ROOM—NIGHT
The front door opening reveals Nan—in street-clothes, wearing coat. We hear Christine:

CHRISTINE'S VOICE: What do *you* want?

As Nan walks into the room, we see Christine—who has opened the door to Nan.

Nan is tensely controlled. Christine masks nervousness at beginning of scene.

NAN: *(following a plan)* I want to know why you called me about Don.

CHRISTINE: Where *is* he? Do you know?

NAN: *(avoids answer)* Why did you say he was in danger?

CHRISTINE: Maybe I meant danger from *me.* I'm said to be a very bad influence on impressionable young men.

NAN: Christine—do you care anything at all about Don?

CHRISTINE: That's—my business. And *his.* I'll tell you one thing. You can't break it up—you might as well quit trying . . .

NAN: *(lets her have it)* There's nothing to break up—now. Don is dead. He was killed by a hit-run driver about two hours ago—right while you were on the 'phone *telling me he was in danger* . . .

During this, shock and stunned hysteria rise in Christine. She bursts out suddenly.

CHRISTINE: *(wildly)* No—you . . . No, they *didn't* . . .

NAN: *Who* didn't? Who was going to kill him? *Who?*

CHRISTINE: I don't know . . .

NAN: Of *course* you know. The police think it was an accident. But you and I know better! Who *was* it?

As she speaks, Christine turns from her blindly.

61

NAN: *(continued)* *(suddenly, moving to 'phone)* If you won't tell *me*—you'll have to tell the *police* . . .

Startling both, 'phone begins to ring—before Nan touches it. Both stare. Then—slowly—Christine achieves partial self-control, lifts receiver.

CHRISTINE: *(answering)* Yes? *(reacts strangely)* No! No—I don't want to talk to him. Don't put any calls through. *No! (hangs up)*

A weird mingling of hysteria and mirthless laughter shows on her face.

A sly, vengeful look of triumph comes in Christine's eyes.

Deliberately, she sets a match to a keg of dynamite.

CHRISTINE: *(continued)* All right. I think I *will* tell you who probably drove the car. The results might be interesting—for a lot of people. His name is Bailey. He runs a shooting-gallery down at the beach. Does their killing on a piecework basis.

NAN: Bailey?

CHRISTINE: Yes—Bailey. Only maybe you won't want to meet him after I tell you something else. *(now it's her turn)* Do you know who that was on the 'phone? Your husband! The great Mr. Bradley Collins! *(hysteria mounting)* Do you know why Don was killed? Because of your husband—the great Mr. Bradley Collins! Because Don found out the great Mr. Bradley Collins is really Frank Johnson—a member of the Communist Party and working for the Party right now . . . !

As she speaks, she draws photostat from drawer—tosses it on desk toward Nan, who stares at it unbelievingly.

INSERT OF PHOTOSTAT

The picture Christine showed to Don: Christine and Brad as lovers.

CHRISTINE'S VOICE: Charming—weren't we? Young love amongst the lower classes? Two bright young Communists—out to save the world!

Back to scene: Now Nan knows all.

CHRISTINE: I was good enough for him then! But I wasn't good enough for Don! All right—I wasn't good enough! So Don's dead! So that's that! Now go on home to your husband! Go on—*Get out!*

She rages toward Nan—almost screaming.
CHRISTINE: *(continued) Get out—get out—get out . . . !*
Not afraid but aware she can accomplish no more here, Nan exits.
Christine slams door violently—turns into camera.
Close shot on Christine. Shuddering—sobbing—last vestiges of control destroyed—she strikes hands against wall and against her face. Suddenly, sobbing stops. Terrible final decision shows in her face and eyes. She starts forward.

INTERIOR LOBBY OF CHRISTINE'S APARTMENT
BUILDING—NIGHT
Desk—small switchboard—elevator in background. Elderly Night Clerk plugs switchboard—listens through headphones.
NIGHT CLERK: I'm sorry, Mr. Collins—but I *cannot* ring Miss Norman's apartment. No, sir. She gave positive orders not to put through any calls. I'd lose my job. *I'm sorry.*
During last of this, Nan appears from elevator. Night Clerk plugs out—sees her—gets up as she approaches.
NIGHT CLERK: Are you Mrs. Bradley Collins?
NAN: *(lifelessly)* Yes—I'm—Mrs. Collins.
NIGHT CLERK: Your husband has been trying to get in touch with you. He said it's very important. *(he completely misreads Nan's reaction to this; well-meaningly)*
NIGHT CLERK: *(continued)* Those little quarrels—we all *have* them. I used to tell my wife—she died several years ago—success in marriage calls for give and take . . . sometimes more give than take . . .
Nan makes a very important decision—interrupts in the middle of this:
NAN: Will you call a cab for me?
NIGHT CLERK: Don't you want to talk to Mr. Collins first?
NAN: No—no, thank you.
NIGHT CLERK: Well—all right. *(returning to switchboard; muttering)* It is too bad—when young people get in arguments . . .
Close shot on Nan. She knows now what she must do.

DISSOLVE

INTERIOR CHRISTINE'S LIVING ROOM—NIGHT

We start in closeup of Christine—as she writes hurriedly, ending several-page suicide note. (We do not insert this note.)

Camera pulls back slowly—revealing microfilms, photostats, Brad's dossier, *other incriminating material piled on desk near Don's framed photograph.*

Christine signs her name. Then Nixon's hand enters shot— closing on her wrist.

Wider angle revealing Nixon. Impassive—amused in his own way—he appraises her stunned reaction to his presence, and her realization of what impends. He picks up the suicide note and reads—mocking inflection underlining key words. Embers burn in fireplace behind him.

NIXON: *(reading)* "To Whom It May Concern: I, Christine Norman, member of the Communist Party—Party Card Number 1179-J— being of sound mind . . ." *(skips over)* . . . and so on and so on . . . *(reading)* "before I die I want to tell the truth about the Communist Party . . ."

He shakes his head almost pityingly.

NIXON: *(continued) (smiling slightly)* Of course. Of course. Under the circumstances—suicide is an excellent solution. But we will have to change some of the details—a little.

Negligently, he tosses suicide note to catch fire and burn on embers.

NIXON: *(continued)* We won't bring politics into it. It is simply a suicide for love. An emotional woman—ill-balanced, as is shown by the fact she fell insanely in love with a man younger in years, infinitely younger in experience. He is accidentally killed. She kills herself. Their case is closed.

Christine rises suddenly—retreats from Nixon—all at once darts toward door. He has anticipated this and moves with surprising speed—seizing her. She struggles violently but he's too strong for her.

EXTERIOR CHRISTINE'S APARTMENT BUILDING— NIGHT

Brad drives in—is forced to park some distance from building entrance because of cars already parked along street. He jumps out—starts toward entrance. Several pedestrians are passing in background.

Suddenly, a woman's terrible scream from high above offstage causes Brad and the others to look straight up out of shot.

Trick shot as if from Brad's angle—delivering effect of Christine's body plummeting down from many stories above.

Flash of Brad's face. Horrified—he doesn't know for an instant that it's not Nan.

Flashes of other horrified faces. Offstage, a crash as the falling body strikes.

Trick shot—actual details masked from camera by people running in, but with effect that Christine's body is impaled on spearpoints of iron fence in front of building.

Close shot on Brad. He recognizes Christine—doesn't know what may have become of Nan. Crowd ad libs come offstage. Brad starts on. Camera pans him to apartment entrance.

INTERIOR LOBBY OF CHRISTINE'S APARTMENT BUILDING—NIGHT

Brad rushes in just as Night Clerk starts out. Almost beside himself, Brad grabs and stops the Night Clerk.

BRAD: Do you know if Mrs. Collins is still up in Miss Norman's apartment?

NIGHT CLERK: Mrs. Collins? Oh—yes. Are you Mr. Collins?

BRAD: Yes! Is she still up there?

NIGHT CLERK: Why, no—no, Mr. Collins. She left about, fifteen minutes ago. She had me call a taxicab for her.

BRAD: Where did she go? Do you know?

NIGHT CLERK: Why—as a matter of fact—yes. That is, I suppose . . . Well . . .

BRAD: *(shaking him)* You suppose *what*!?

NIGHT CLERK: Well—you know how women are when they're angry . . .

BRAD: *Where did she go!?*

65

NIGHT CLERK: Why, she—*please*, Mr. Collins—you're *hurting me*—she told the driver to take her to Bailey's shooting-gallery, at the Beach. *(babbling)* I couldn't imagine a nice woman—alone—going to a place like that at this time of night . . .
Brad throws him away as he speaks—turns and hurries out.

DISSOLVE

EXTERIOR SHOOTING GALLERY—NIGHT
Close shot on a Pretty Girl—who fires rifle straight into camera. Bailey's arms come in—encircling Girl at shoulders, as his hands close over hers on rifle.
BAILEY'S VOICE: You need practice, baby. You need a *lot* of practice.
Wider angle delivers Bailey—and the Girl's escort, a young Sailor, who commands resentfully:
SAILOR: Hey—take your paws off of her!
Bailey pulls trigger and hits offstage target—takes his time about releasing Girl.
BAILEY: *(over shoulder to Sailor)* What's a matter, Sailor? Can't stand competition? *(to Girl)* You could do better, baby. You could do better.
She half-likes this. Sailor steers her away angrily. Bailey grins. Camera pans with him. Now he sees Nan in corner—just firing last shot in rifle. She puts gun down—looks aside at Bailey. During ensuing—in background—we establish Bailey's pal, Grip Wilson, who operates a wheel-of-fortune booth.
NAN: How many shots do these things hold?
BAILEY: *(reacting to her)* Why—six, baby—six. Have six on the house.
He hands her another rifle. Just as she starts to fire:
JEB'S VOICE: Change, please—Mr. Bailey.
Closeup of Nan—looking after Bailey, offstage. She realizes this is the man Christine Norman said killed Don. She starts firing at offstage target viciously.
Close shot on Jeb and Bailey—who makes change from cash-register on counter. Gunshots are heard offstage.

66

JEB: *(indicating Nan)* What's a beautiful dame like that doin' down here?

BAILEY: Maybe she heard about me.

JEB: You ain't *that* good!

BAILEY: Oh, no?

> *He exits back toward Nan.*
> *Close shot on Nan. She fires a shot as Bailey enters. He puts arms around her shoulders, controlling the rifle—speaks exactly as he spoke to the Girl earlier:*

BAILEY: You need practice, baby. You need a *lot* of practice.

> *He can't see the expression that we see on Nan's face. He repels her but she forces herself to play up. He fires with her. We hear bong! as shot hits target.*

BAILEY: *(continued)* See how I mean?

NAN: *(pretends awe)* Why—that's wonderful.

BAILEY: *(arms still around her)* All you need is a teacher. *(prepares to fire again)* And—baby—can I teach! *(fires; hits offstage target again)* All you gotta do is squeeze it gentle.

> *Now at last he releases her—puts gun down on counter.*

BAILEY: *(continued)* Who d'ya wanta kill?

NAN: Why—nobody.

BAILEY: Quit kiddin'. Who you mad at?

NAN: Who said I was mad?

BAILEY: You gotta be. And it's gotta be a guy you're mad at. Always is.

NAN: You know all the answers—don't you, Mr. Bailey?

BAILEY: Sure. Y' know—good-lookin' babe like you can't go wanderin' around alone, down here. It's against the law. And a waste of talent. Where to, baby?

NAN: Why—I was thinking of going home. Only he might be there waiting.

BAILEY: So we'll take a little detour on the way. *(calls offstage)* Hey—Grip.

> *Close shot on Grip. He spins wheel-of-fortune—stops it on* Grand Prize—*while he speaks.*

GRIP: Yeah—*I* know. Anybody wants you—you'll be at the usual place.

Close shot on Nan and Bailey.
NAN: Your—friend seems to know some answers, too.
BAILEY: Could be. *(to Jeb in background)* Take over. An' keep your mitts out of the till or I'll stomp on 'em!
NAN: You're—very tough—aren't you?
BAILEY: Only in business, baby. Never when I'm out for pleasure.
He starts her away.

DISSOLVE

EXTERIOR STREET SIGN—NIGHT
Reading "INTERNATIONAL SETTLEMENT." *If a stock shot is available showing background of flashing signs and honky-tonks, so much the better.*

DISSOLVE THROUGH TO
A neon sign—"GAY PAREE." *Music coming offstage.*

DISSOLVE THROUGH TO INTERIOR HONKY-TONK—NIGHT
Dim lighting, garish decoration and a tiny stage on which a piano player and violinist are trying to be heard above the din.
We start on excessively-clothed, much-madeup Girl who is beginning a walk-around routine. Camera sweep establishes noisy, crowded joint—frequented by dockworkers and their women, and so forth. Shot ends on Nan and Bailey, seated in a booth. They have drinks before them. Bailey drains his glass—studies Nan. He's no fool despite his conceit.
BAILEY: Tell me about it.
NAN: Tell you—what?
BAILEY: Look, baby—highclass merchandise don't have to go around lookin' for a market. So a guy stood you up? So what? You could get a new one right in your own backyard. Didn't hafta come slummin'—just to find yourself good company.
NAN: You're—clever, aren't you?
BAILEY: I ain't dumb. You an' me didn't meet just by accident.
NAN: *(oddly)* I—don't believe in accidents.

68

BAILEY: Smart kid.
He drains his drink—indicates.
BAILEY: *(continued)* Drink up, baby. It comes from a pump.
He beckons offstage. Nan sips drink—hates it—but under his gaze empties the glass. Waiter Girl enters.
BAILEY: *(continued)* Two more of the same.
NAN: Doubled.
Bailey reacts to this. Things are going great. He gestures for Waiter Girl to exit—studies Nan—goes back to the point:
BAILEY: What're you after that ain't for laughs?
NAN: I'm—not sure I ought to trust you . . .
BAILEY: Treated you okay so far—haven't I? Come on, baby—lay it on the well-known line.
Close shot on Nan. She knows she's playing with dynamite—tries to make every word and implication count.
NAN: Well, I—well, to be honest about it—a friend of mine has a problem. She's married . . .
BAILEY: She's got a problem, baby—she's got a problem! And so?
NAN: *(inventing as she goes along)* Well, her husband drinks. And he beats her. He's—just no good. But he has a lot of life insurance.
BAILEY: Oh—oh. One of them! *(suddenly)* Hold it, baby.
He indicates warningly. Waiter Girl enters with drinks. Bailey fumbles in pockets—can't find enough money—produces wallet and starts showing the crisp big bills we saw Nixon give him.
BAILEY: *(continued) (to Waiter Girl)* Can you break a C-note?
WAITER GIRL: *(typically)* I can fracture it. How d'ya want your change—in nickels?
BAILEY: Go on—go on!
Waiter Girl exits. Bailey studies Nan probingly.
BAILEY: *(continued) (after moment)* Who sent you to me?
Nan is prepared for this attack—answers cross-examination with half-truth.
NAN: Let's say—a former client of yours.
BAILEY: Who?
NAN: I'll have to know you a whole lot better—before I tell you that.
Waiter Girl enters with drinks—and Bailey's change, most of which he stuffs in pocket. He gives Waiter Girl a big bill as tip.

BAILEY: Go on—go on.
As Waiter Girl exits

DISSOLVE

EXTERIOR SHOOTING GALLERY—NIGHT
Brad enters. The gallery has a small rush of customers. Jeb is confusedly busy loading guns—collecting coins.
After a moment, Jeb gets to Brad—automatically sliding rifle along counter to him.
JEB: Six shots for a quarter—twelve for thirty-fi' cents.
BRAD: Where's Bailey?
JEB: Bailey? He's gone for the night.
BRAD: Was there a woman with him?
JEB: I—ain't supposed to talk about Mr. Bailey's private affairs.
He sees a customer—moves away. Grimly, Brad produces a bill. When Jeb returns:
BRAD: *Was there a woman with him?*
Jeb pockets bill quickly—then stalls.
JEB: Now—lemme see . . .
BRAD: *Was there a woman with him?*
JEB: Oh—sure—always is.
BRAD: Where did they go?
JEB: Well—hard to say. That Bailey—he sure gits around. *(chuckles)* Sure gits the women, too!
Brad can stand no more. He reaches—grabs Jeb's shirtfront—yanks him violently.
BRAD: *This one happens to be my wife!* Where did he take her?
Shot over Grip—in wheel-of-fortune booth. He spins wheel for benefit of two customers—has heard Brad ask about Nan—steps to wall-'phone and dials, keeping his eyes on Brad.
Close shot on Brad and Jeb—who struggles and gasps.
JEB: Leggo! Leggo o' me! How would I know? He's got hangouts all over town. *Leggo!*
Brad releases him. Jeb sways back from Brad.
Close shot on Grip. A voice comes over 'phone:
VOICE ON 'PHONE: *J. T. Arnold—Import-Export . . .*

70

GRIP: *(on 'phone)* This is Grip Wilson down at the Beach. Yeah . . .

INTERIOR PARTY ROOM INNER OFFICE—NIGHT
Arnold stands by. Nixon listens to Grip over 'phone. Garth—the bodyguard—is in background as usual.
NIXON: *(on 'phone)* Where did Bailey take Mrs. Collins?
GRIP'S VOICE: *(over 'phone)* Gay Paree—in the International Settlement.
NIXON: I see. Now listen to me. Listen carefully.

EXTERIOR SHOOTING GALLERY—NIGHT
Close shot on Brad.
JEB: *(aggrievedly)* If I don't know—I can't tell you—can I?
He turns to wait on another customer. Brad glowers—helplessly—turns to exit. Camera pans and picks up Grip—moving to intercept Brad.
GRIP: *(with fake casualness)* Hi—Mr. Collins. Lookin' for somebody?
BRAD: Your pal—Bailey.
GRIP: Oh—yeah. Well—I could probably take you to him. Only I lose money closin' up early. How much is it worth to you?
Brad is tempted to slug—but for Nan's sake maintains control. He produces several bills—which Grip grabs.
GRIP: *(continued)* Sure want him bad—don't you? Okay. C'm'on.
He leads Brad away as we

DISSOLVE

INTERIOR HONKY-TONK—NIGHT
Nan and Bailey are dancing. He holds her very close.
BAILEY: Like me—huh, baby?
NAN: Oh—very much.
BAILEY: Ain't enough.
NAN: Well—after all—I have to get used to you.
BAILEY: That ain't hard. *(after moment)* This guy with the life insurance—he ain't married to a *friend* of yours. Married to *you*. You're the girl wants to be a rich widow.

71

NAN: Now—wouldn't I be a sucker to say "Yes" to that?

BAILEY: *I'm* no sucker, baby.

A towering Tough taps Bailey on shoulder.

TOUGH: How 'bout me cuttin' in, Mac?

BAILEY: Yeah—how about it?

He releases Nan and in continuing move drives a brutal blow into Tough's belly—clips him on chin as he doubles over—drops him on floor—resumes embrace and dances on with Nan.

BAILEY: *(continued)* See what I mean, baby?

NAN: Very neat. But not very smart.

She disengages herself—starts move back to booth. Camera pans with them. Nan reaches booth—sits down. Bailey slides in beside her instead of sitting down across from her.

NAN: *(continued)* Insurance companies don't pay off on strong-arm stuff. Only on—accidents.

BAILEY: Thought you didn't believe in accidents.

NAN: I don't. Insurance companies do. If they're accidental enough. Only—you wouldn't know how to make it look good.

BAILEY: Oh—no? A thousand bucks and a pretty smile—an' you an' me would be in business.

NAN: But there'd have to be a plan—some special way . . .

BAILEY: Maybe there is, baby—maybe there is!

NAN: You talk like you'd done some of these jobs before.

BAILEY: Maybe I have, baby—maybe I have.

His arm slides around her shoulders. She tightens involuntarily but submits to this during ensuing.

NAN: Let's see your clippings.

BAILEY: Huh?

NAN: Prove it to me.

BAILEY: *(drains another drink)* Well, baby—I ain't sayin' this happened—I'm only sayin' it could of. Take for instance there's a smart G that gets an accident deal. What does he do? Simple. Steals an old jalopy—stakes out in a certain place 'til a certain guy comes along—gives her the gas—wham! Funny thing—this certain guy gets taken down dead *by accident . . .*

At end of this, he has broken himself up with drunken, jeering laughter.

72

Closeup of Nan. Bailey's continuing laughter coming offstage. Now she knows Bailey killed her brother.

BAILEY'S VOICE: *(broken by continuing laughter)* This friend of mine drives the jalopy off the dock—into the bay. No evidence. No nothin'. Accident . . .

Shot over Arnold—just inside entrance. We see and hear Bailey laughing, in booth in background.

ARNOLD: *(to Waiter Girl; indicating Bailey)* Get him over here. In a hurry.

EXTERIOR SALOON—NIGHT

This is the exterior of a dingy-looking drinking place. Brad and Grip come out.

GRIP: Funny how he don't seem to be around no place. Tell you, though—Mr. Collins—there's another joint he goes to, down by the docks . . .

BRAD: You've led me around by the nose long enough.

Suddenly without warning—Brad grabs Grip, whirls him into an alley-mouth. Brad's blows pin Grip to the wall. He's sinking down when Brad grabs, yanks him up, and demands:

BRAD: *(continued)* Where are they? Come on! *Where are they?*

Stunned and scared, Grip tries to break free. Brad's punch to body drops him in heap—in darkness. Sound of Brad's continued punishment of Grip as he demands:

BRAD: *(continued) Where are they?*

GRIP: *(gasping)* Don't hit me again. I—can't take it. *(as Brad starts punch)* I'll tell you . . . !

INTERIOR HONKY-TONK—NIGHT

Bailey and Arnold in foreground look toward Nan who's still in booth in background.

BAILEY: Look, I—I never saw the dame before. How would *I* know who she is?

ARNOLD: You're a drunken fool. The only chance you have is to do exactly as you're told—and do it in a hurry!

BAILEY: Sure—sure.

He moves away quickly to rejoin Nan.

Close shot on Nan. She watches Bailey approaching offstage. She'd like to get out—doesn't know how to manage it.

BAILEY: *(entering; nodding over shoulder)* Old pal of mine. Tipped me off about a new spot that just opened. Hot as a firecracker. What he tells me, baby—you wouldn't wanta miss it.

NAN: I—ought to be getting home.

BAILEY: Now—baby—whata you wanta go *home* for? You wanta see the sights. Besides—you an' me got some business to wind up. C'm'on!

She hesitates visibly. His hand closes on her arm. He brings her up. Camera pans them toward exit.

Shot over Arnold—his back to camera—watching Bailey and Nan exiting. When they're gone, he starts toward telephone at far end of bar. But a Drunk and his Girl anticipate Arnold's move. Drunk makes delaying business of fumbling before dialing correct number. He keeps his arm around Girl. Arnold waits impatiently.

DRUNK: *(finally, on 'phone)* Hello—Rose? Rose, I'm still stuck at the office. Yeah—takin' inventory. Naw—I can't say when I'll be home—because I don't *know* when . . .

During this, his Girl offers a drink. He gulps before continuing.

DRUNK: *(continued)* Now—Rose—you *know* I'd sooner be with my dear little wifey—but I'm a busy man . . . *(with sudden anger)* Ahh—shuddup! An' the same to you!

He bangs receiver—jostles Arnold, who glowers.

DRUNK: *(continued)* *(while Arnold dials)* You're wastin' your time, Mac! The old hag'll call yuh a liar even if you tell her the truth! Happens to the best of us!

Arnold scowls at him. The Girl grabs Drunk, yanks him back to stool, as we hear:

VOICE ON 'PHONE: *J. T. Arnold—Import-Export.*

Close shot on Arnold—who speaks very quietly.

ARNOLD: This is Mr. Arnold. That shipment we discussed is on the way over. It should be delivered within the next twenty minutes. Yes.

Suddenly, hand in a man's side-pocket—holding gun—thrusts in against small of Arnold's back.

BRAD'S VOICE: *(stopping Arnold's turn)* If you don't think it's a real gun—Mr. Arnold—yell and find out.
Arnold freezes.
Wider angle reveals Brad—so close to Arnold's back that no bystander would observe gun he keeps hidden in pocket.
BRAD: But you're a businessman. You know better than to bet on long-shots.
Arnold shows physical cowardice—doesn't dare look over shoulder.
BRAD: *(continued)* Walk on out. Slow.
Arnold obeys. Camera pans them toward exit. To those they pass, they appear to be two friends walking out together. As they disappear

DISSOLVE

WHARF (BETHLEHEM STEEL)—NIGHT
Brad drives his car in through maze of cranes, and stops car in front of metal roller doors of warehouse.
(Note: This is same setup as in Scene 39—in which Brad arrived at Party headquarters the first time.)

DOORKEEPER'S BOX (BETHLEHEM STEEL)—NIGHT
As in Scene 39, the Lookout—Burke—peers through window and flashes light.

INTERIOR CAR (BETHLEHEM STEEL)—NIGHT
Circle of light strikes on Brad and Arnold. Brad holds gun low—out of Lookout's range of vision—against Arnold's side.
BRAD: *(quiet; deadly)* Tell him Nixon sent you to bring me in.
Arnold hesitates.
BRAD: *(continued)* Go on!
ARNOLD: *(in terror)* It's—all right. I was—sent to bring him in.
Brief pause for suspense. Then light snaps off. Brad drives one-handed—keeps gun against Arnold. Car idles on into warehouse. Roller doors close.

75

INTERIOR PARTY ROOM—NIGHT
Nan and Bailey stand facing Nixon—seated behind table, interrogating them.

NIXON: *(checks notes before him; speaks as of Nan)* You took a taxicab from Christine Norman's apartment at 10:17. *(queries)* What time was it when you met Bailey? *(she stands mute; he repeats to Bailey)* What time was it?

BAILEY: Ten-forty.

NIXON: Are you positive?

BAILEY: Yeah. I looked at my watch just a minute before she showed up.

Bailey is on the spot and sweating. Nan is the helpless target. Nixon is impassive—as when he grilled Ralston.

NIXON: *(again to Nan)* Then you went direct to the Beach. There wouldn't have been time for you to stop anywhere—for example to telephone the police.

She still stands mute. Nixon studies her momentarily.

NIXON: *(continued) (resumes to Bailey)* Could she have telephoned after you met?

BAILEY: I was with her every minute.

NIXON: You're sure?

BAILEY: Yeah—I'm sure! She was so busy workin' on me she wouldn't of left me if I asked her to.

INTERIOR ELEVATOR—NIGHT
Elevator is moving up. Brad keeps Arnold covered. We establish light-switch near elevator push-button.

Suddenly, Arnold takes desperate chance—snaps light off and in continuing movement attacks Brad.

They struggle furiously, almost in silence. It's too dark for details. Brad slugs—breaks free—slugs again. Elevator stops with jerk. Brad starts out alone. Arnold's body is crumpled on elevator floor.

INTERIOR PARTY ROOM—NIGHT
Close shot on Nan. She's controlled—coldly defiant.

NAN: Why don't you get to the point!?

76

NIXON: *(unaffected)* We've come to the point—Mrs. Collins. Not that you know who killed your brother—but that you know *why* he was killed. Because he found out your husband is a Communist—obeying Party orders in the waterfront negotiations. I had to make sure—obviously—that you hadn't communicated that knowledge to anyone else. I'm satisfied now that you haven't. That's all I wanted from you. *(pointedly)* Christine Norman committed suicide—shortly after you left her—in grief because of your brother's death.

Nan reacts in shock.

NIXON: *(continued)* You're going to do the same thing, Mrs. Collins. Mrs. Collins is the only witness against you, Bailey.

Bailey's reaction tells everything. He hates Nan—will get sadistic pleasure from silencing her. He starts move. She flinches slightly. Nixon watches passionlessly.

INTERIOR PARTY ROOM INNER OFFICE—NIGHT

In dim light, we see Brad climbing through the high interior light. Brad crosses toward connecting door to outer office.

Nan's scream is heard offstage.

Closeup of Brad. We read on his face reaction to statements that up to this moment might have come close to the ugly truth. If he still loved success more than anything else, he'd turn and leave now.

NIXON'S VOICE: Of course—your husband will know it wasn't a suicide. But if you think he'll do anything about it—you're wrong. He was able to forget about Christine Norman. He'll be able to forget about *you.*

Brad's decision is shown as his face hardens. He starts forward—gun lifting.

INTERIOR PARTY ROOM—NIGHT

Nan fights against Bailey—who whirls her toward door, enjoying fact he's hurting her.

BRAD'S VOICE: Nan!

Another angle revealing Brad—who covers Bailey with gun. Nixon never moves. Nan fights free from Bailey's grasp.

BRAD: *(nods over shoulder into inner office)* There's a 'phone in here. Call the police.

> *Staring at Brad, Nan moves toward door to inner office. He steps aside just enough to let her pass.*

NIXON: *(to Nan)* Mrs. Collins—if you call the police, your husband will be arrested for murder.

> *As Nan hesitates:*

BRAD: *(curtly commanding)* Get on the 'phone. *Go on!*

> *She moves past him—disappearing into inner office.*

NIXON: Johnson! Even if you kill me—which is what you want to do—your complete record will still be delivered to the F.B.I. You have absolutely nothing to gain—everything to lose ...

> *During this, he makes typical business of taking cigarette from his leather case that lies on desk. He lights cigarette—puffs— while he speaks.*

BRAD: I lost anything I had—the day you walked in on me with that Commy Party card. *(commanding)* Now get on your feet!

> *Seemingly defeated, Nixon prepares unhurriedly to obey.*
>
> *Close shot on Nixon. He makes such casual business of closing cigarette-case and starting to return it to his inside coat-pocket while he rises—that we have no suspicion of what's coming: His eyes are on Brad offstage.*

NIXON: *(as he rises)* Very well. *(an apparent confession of cynical surrender)* That's the difficulty with people like you, Johnson. Too emotional for Party purposes. You all want to be martyrs ...

> *This covers*

NAN'S VOICE: Hello. Police Department ... ?

> *Nixon's hand inside coat puts cigarette case in pocket—and in continuing smooth move whips gun from shoulder-holster—of which we get flash as he draws and in same instant fires at Brad offstage.*
>
> *Shot over Nixon. Brad is hit in body—staggers—for a split second off-guard. In this instant, Bailey hurls himself at Brad. Nixon rushes in. Brad smashes gun-barrel across Bailey's face—knocking him back against Nixon. In continuing move, Brad whirls through doorway into inner office—slams door. Nixon fires through door.*

INTERIOR PARTY ROOM INNER OFFICE—NIGHT

NAN: *(on phone)* Yes—the J. T. Arnold Import-Export Warehouse
... Yes. Hurry!

During this, Brad shoves desk against door—which opens in. Gunshots rip through door panels—missing him. He grabs Nan—starts her out through interior window by which he entered.

INTERIOR PARTY ROOM—NIGHT

Close shot on Nixon and Bailey battering at door.

INTERIOR THIRD FLOOR OF WAREHOUSE (BETHLEHEM STEEL)—NIGHT

Nan and Brad run down from fourth floor. But on the third floor—suddenly—he stops her.

WHAT THEY SEE:

Garth comes running up stairway toward them—gun in hand. He fires.

Brad and Nan. He pulls her off the landing—into the third floor of warehouse.

Close shot on Nixon and Bailey. Nixon sees Brad and Nan below offstage. He starts Bailey on—firing as they go.

Long shot—as gunfire comes over. A flash of Nan and Brad disappearing into shadows at the other end of warehouse.

SECTION OF WAREHOUSE (STUDIO)—NIGHT

*Note: This is a studio reproduction of a small section of the warehouse. It consists of a photo backing in front of which are bales of the type that would normally be found in an import-export warehouse. A couple of cargo-hooks are spiked in these—*important for an ensuing scene.

Close shot on Nan and Brad. For first time, Nan realizes Brad is wounded. Blood shows through his sleeve. They're hidden behind the boxes and bales.

NAN: Brad—why didn't you tell me? Why didn't you come to me and tell me?

BRAD: *(with harsh self-condemnation)* I didn't want you to know what the great Bradley Collins really was—what he *is* . . .
His confession breaks off suddenly.

INTERIOR THIRD FLOOR WAREHOUSE (BETHLEHEM STEEL)—NIGHT
Nixon, Bailey and Garth come down the warehouse—guns in hands—straight toward where Brad and Nan are hidden.
Close shot on Brad and Nan.
BRAD: *(suddenly)* . . . But I loved you. Don't ever doubt that. Don't ever forget it. *(reacts to what he sees offstage)* Stay here.
He starts out—to divert pursuit from her.
NAN: Brad . . . !
He runs on.
Long shot of Brad racing across warehouse—disappearing in shadows—then reappearing for flash as he runs in.
Flashes of the Communists as they fire at him.
Long shot of Brad disappearing into absolute darkness. He fires.
Communists scatter for cover.
Close shot on Garth. He starts cautiously forward, moves along row of boxes and bales—toward Brad offstage.
Flash of Brad. He sees Garth offstage—lifts gun.
Flash of Garth. He fires. At same instant, Brad fires from offstage. Garth is hit—crumples.
Flash of Nixon and Bailey. They fire at Brad—who isn't seen. His answering single gunshot gives his location.
Close shot on Brad. Answering offstage shots shatter some convenient prop just as he ducks from original position.
Close shot on Nixon. He ducks in shadows—disappears.
Close shot on Brad. He comes out of shadows—fires.
Flash of Bailey.
He's hit—falls, dying.
Flash of Brad.
He sees Bailey fall. But where is Nixon? He looks around and suddenly reacts to what he sees:
Panning shot of Nixon slipping along from one shadow to the next. Then as camera pans, we see the pile of boxes and bales and know he's somewhere near Nan.

Close shot on Brad. He sees Nixon offstage nearing Nan—starts to her rescue.

Close shot on Nan. A figure rises slowly in shadows behind her.

Close shot—revealing that the figure is Nixon. He aims at Nan.

Panning shot of Brad.

The camera sweeps him toward Nixon and Nan. He pulls trigger. Gun is empty. He flings it aside.

Nixon sees Brad—whirls from Nan and fires. Shot hits Brad in body—staggers him. But he stumbles on. Nixon fires again. This time, he misses.

Brad throws himself headlong at Nixon. The two men fall fighting viciously. Nixon loses his gun.

INSERT OF GUN

as it spins across floor and comes to rest not far from edge of the well.

Close shot on Brad and Nixon.

His wounds weaken Brad. Nixon is in better position. He rises a split second before Brad and slugs Brad (back to camera) as Brad lurches up.

Close shot on Brad falling backward heavily—almost at Nan's feet.

Close shot on Nixon bending to pick up the gun.

Close shot on Brad as he rises and charges past camera toward Vorak.

Flash of Nixon—firing.

Flash of Brad hit again—but surging on with berserk fury.

Flash of Nixon firing again at man who can't be stopped. He backs toward well. Fear shows in Nixon for first time.

Flash of Brad knocked backward by bullet—against boxes and bales. His hand strikes against cargo-hook spiked in bale. Wild grin of recognition shows on his blood-marked face. He yanks cargo-hook free—starts throw.

Flash of Nixon firing—just as cargo-hook flashes in. The needle-point drives into his body, and he is hurled backward. Gun falls from his hand.

Flash of Brad dying on his feet—somehow continuing toward Nan.

Shot at edge of well. Nixon (double) staggers backward past camera—clawing at cargo-hook in his breast. He hits railing— topples over—screaming as he falls.

Shot—shooting up from ground floor.

Nixon (dummy) comes hurtling down—past camera.

INTERIOR SECTION OF WAREHOUSE (STUDIO)— NIGHT

Full shot centering on Brad—who half sits, half lies on floor. Nan, Jim Travis and Police Doctor are close by Brad. There are half a dozen uniformed policemen in the shot. Garth—wounded and a prisoner—is being led off.

Close shot on Brad, Nan and Jim. Police Doctor—having done all he can for Brad, steps back offstage.

BRAD: *(speaks slowly, with difficulty; to Jim)* Everything you—need to stop the—tieup—in Nixon's office . . .

JIM: Brad—don't try to talk any more.

BRAD: *(ghostly grin)* Have to. Unfinished business to—clear up . . . *(rallying)* Nan made a mistake. But that can be—fixed. Take care of her—Jim . . .

NAN: *(fighting sobs)* Brad—I love *you*—I'll always love you . . .

BRAD: Always—long time, honey. Too long. Jim's—right man for you. Always was . . .

Jim draws back offstage. Camera moves in on Brad and Nan.

BRAD: *(continued) (grins; dying)* I—always told you—you came along too late for me . . .

He dies. Nan holds him close as we

FADE OUT

THE END